Building Unique and Useful Kids' Furniture

24 Great Do-It-Yourself Projects

by Spike Carlsen

LINDEN PUBLISHING

Fresno

Building Unique and Useful Kids' Furniture
24 Great Do-It-Yourself Projects
by Spike Carlsen

ISBN: 978-1-610353-25-0
135798642

DISCLAIMER: Woodworking is inherently dangerous. Your safety
is your responsibility. Neither Linden Publishing nor the author
assume any responsibility for any injuries or accidents.

Book design by Maura J. Zimmer
Cover design by Jim Goold

Printed in the United States of America

Library of Congress Cataloging-in-Publication Data on file

The Woodworker's Library
Linden Publishing Co. Inc.
2006 S. Mary
Fresno, CA 93721
www.lindenpub.com

About This Book

Every "how-to" book is a compromise between how many projects to squeeze in and how much detail to delve into. This book tried to strike a logical balance. With YouTube at one's disposal, one can find tutorials on just about anything. So when it came to more advanced techniques—using a biscuit joiner or pocket screw jig—we covered the basics, but encourage you to hit the Internet to learn more.

In the area of plans we tried to provide complete information via diagrams, templates, cutting lists and shopping lists. That said, we encourage you to use our plans as a starting point for creating your own unique furniture. Before digging in, noodle around a bit with the size, color and wood species—then have at it.

A Word on Safety

Woodworking is both intrinsically rewarding and inherently dangerous; before diving into any project, make certain you're comfortable with the tools and materials you'll be handling and take time to familiarize yourself with the overall game plan. Think about safety, not just while a project is being built, but also when it's installed and in use. Use common sense. When in doubt...don't do it.

Dedication

Dedicated to grandchildren everywhere; mine happen to be named Paige, Morgan, Riley, Anna, Claire, Bella, Louise, Priya and Blue.

p. 105

p. 69

p. 83

p. 30

p. 115

Contents

Building Unique, Useful Kids' Furniture

That's the thing about handmade items. They still have the person's mark on them, and when you hold them, you feel less alone. —Aimee Bender

A quote like that packs a pretty powerful punch—and it's true. Even years after it's been created, handmade furniture calls out, "Hey, remember I love you so much I took the time to build this for you."

I became a fan of hand-built kids' stuff one Christmas morning, when, granddaughter Anna—surrounded by piles of plastic toys and games that beeped—was most enthralled by a simple wood circus car I'd made (you can see a similar one on page 24). Built from four store-bought wheels, a couple of 1x6s and a few dowels, I could see her mind churn as she placed a stuffed animal into it and paraded around the room. One moment she was a lion tamer, the next a train engineer. And she didn't do this for minutes—she did it for months. When she outgrew the circus car, her little sister adopted it.

The circus car didn't come with instructions, so she had to make up her own "rules." It was nearly indestructible so she could drag it down the stairs and sit on it without fear of it breaking. And—though I don't think it was clear in her 18-month old mind—somewhere in that little noggin she realized it was made with love by "Poppy."

As the years rolled on, I made more and more furniture. Building things gave me reason to pursue the hobby I loved. It tucked a few extra dollars in my pocket and gave me bragging rights. It gave kids something that was personal and fostered creativity. It gave parents something that didn't have a jillion pieces. I built LEGO tables, toy boxes, dollhouses, sleeping lofts, rocking horses, tree houses, Barbie Doll bunk beds, clothes giraffes and more. And most of those things are still around today.

This book is for those that believe "'tis more blessed to build than to buy." The 24+ projects in this book cast a wide net. They can be used by infants, toddlers, kids and tweens. They can be built by first timers, intermediate do-it-yourselfers and seasoned woodworkers. The projects can be used in bedrooms, kitchens, playrooms and outdoors. Many can be converted to "adult use" when their "kid use" days are past. Better yet, this book doesn't just show you how to build furniture, it shows you how to become a better woodworker.

So, whether your first project is a circus wagon or a bunk bed, roll up your sleeves and get going. You'll make a mark on someone.

—Spike Carlsen

An "Awesome" Mirror

A project to make you go in circles

The full length "I Can Do Anything" mirror (p. 69) is ideal for bedrooms; it fits nicely on the back of a door or on a wall. But what about a mirror for the bathroom? Or above the dresser? Or in the entryway? A person needs to reflect on inspirational things in those places too. So we designed this 2-foot diameter "Born to be AWESOME" mirror for smaller spaces.

We encourage you to customize your mirror, graphics and words so they fit the kid or the family in your life. In fact, for this one, we don't even include a diagram or materials list—so design away! Ours is for a kid that loves skateboarding...and who was, clearly, "born to be awesome."

How to Build It

For starters, don't freak out about the jig in Photo 2. This "trammel jig" can help you cut near-perfect circles, but—if you don't feel like building a jig—cut your parts the good old-fashioned way: freehand.

We started with a 16" diameter mirror which established the basic design. The mirror opening couldn't exceed 15" in diameter, since the face (A) needs to overlap the mirror by at least ½" on all sides. Then a 24" overall diameter allowed us to make good use of material and provided a wide rim for decals.

Layout your ¼" face plywood (A) as shown in Photo 1. We indented the 15" circular opening in a couple of places to allow room for the jumping boys. Cut out the basic shape using a jigsaw and soften the edges with sandpaper.

Next, cut the mirror surround (B) to shape as shown in Photo 2. We made ours from ¹⁄₁₆" Masonite; a material the same thickness as the mirror. The outer diameter needs to be the same as the outer diameter of the face plywood (A) and the inner diameter needs to be the same as that of the mirror. You can use a "trammel jig" as we explain in the sidebar. Or you can cut freehand. Either way, use a new (never-been-bent), fine tooth, rigid jigsaw blade for best results. Older or coarser

1 **DETERMINE** the size and shape of your mirror. Swing the appropriate size circles, then fiddle around with words and images until you're satisfied.

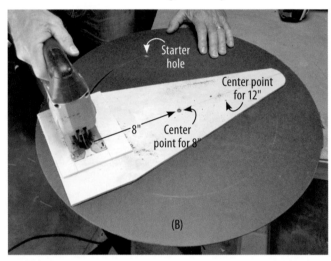

2 **CUT** the three mirror parts—face, surround, and backing (all seen in next photo)—with a jigsaw. For information on the trammel jig shown, see the sidebar.

Cutting with a Trammel Jig

To make the trammel jig, position your jigsaw near the outer edge of a pyramid-shaped piece of plywood, cutting a hole for the blade first. Surround the base of your jigsaw with plywood to hold it firmly in place. Drill center holes 8" and 12" away from the edge of your blade. Use the 12" center hole when cutting the outside perimeter and the 8" center hole when cutting the inside of part B. As you come full circle on the inner circle, move slowly; near the end your center point will float free and you'll have to finish the last stretch freehand.

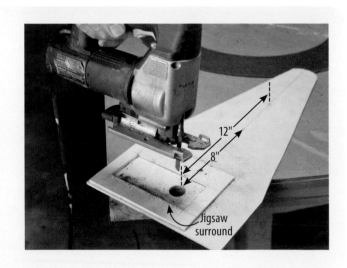

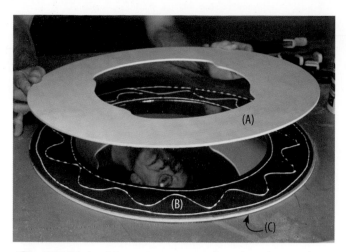

3 GLUE the Masonite surround to the plywood backing, then the face plywood to the surround. Use lots of clamps to hold the parts tightly together until the glue sets.

4 INSTALL the decals after applying a coat of poly or paint to the mirror face. The masking tape keeps the mirror free of drips and glops when finish is applied.

blades will tend to cut an ever-increasing angle as they cut their way around.

Cut the 24" diameter backing piece (C) from ¼" plywood. Glue your mirror "sandwich" together as shown in Photo 3. Use clamps—lots of them—to hold the three parts together until

the glue sets. Apply a coat of water- or oil-based poly and let it dry, then apply the decals. See the "I Can Do Anything" mirror for information on finding and printing the words and images.

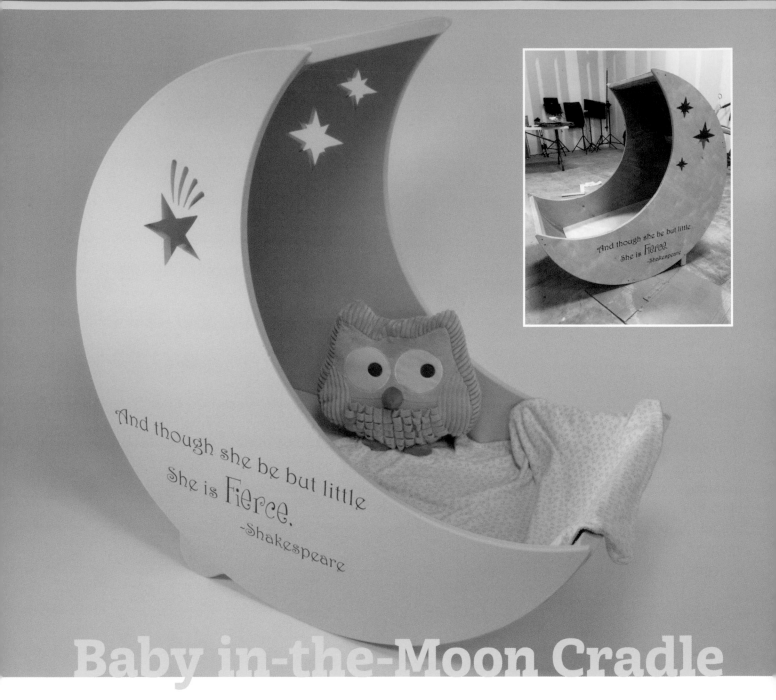

And though she be but little
She is Fierce.
-Shakespeare

Baby in-the-Moon Cradle

A heavenly haven for newborns

This cradle doesn't offer a touch of whimsy—it offers an entire universe of it. But it also has a practical side: It rocks, you can hang mobiles from the tip of the moon and you can lift out the bottom platform to stow things.

Believe it or not, when baby outgrows the moon, youngsters can continue to use it as a cave (upside down), as a space age desk (on its side) or—with caution— as a rocking and rolling gaming chair (right side up, again). We tried them all—and they all worked.

Figure 1

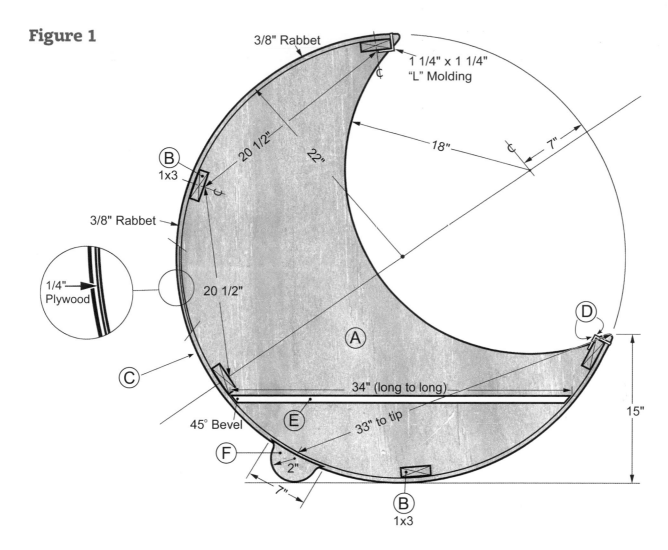

3/8" Rabbet

1 1/4" x 1 1/4" "L" Molding

20 1/2"

22"

18"

7"

Ⓑ
1x3

3/8" Rabbet

1/4" Plywood

20 1/2"

Ⓒ

Ⓐ

Ⓓ

34" (long to long)

15"

45° Bevel

Ⓔ

33" to tip

Ⓕ

2"

7"

Ⓑ
1x3

Fear Not the Curves

When you look at the photos of this finished cradle, you might think "This looks simple to build." When you look at the how-to photos you might think, "*Wow*, this looks way out of my league." The truth lies somewhere in between.

There are only about a dozen pieces—but they have to be cut and assembled carefully. You can do this—just put on your meticulous hat! Once the sides (A) are laid out, cut out and routed you're halfway home. In the "Perfect Circles" sidebar (p. 8) we show you how to cut flawless curves with a router, trammel jig and tracing bit, *but you can cut both sides with your good old jigsaw* as shown in Photo 2. You'll still need a router to cut the rabbets shown in Photo 3, but you don't need the jig or tracing bit shown in the sidebar to build this cradle.

Cutting List

Part	Dimensions	Qty
(A) Sides	¾" x 44" x 44" plywood	2
(B) Ribs	¾" x 2½" x 20" pine	5
(C) Curved back	¼" x 20⅝" x 8' lauan plywood	1
(D) Edge trim	1⅛" x 20⅝" corner molding	2
(E) Bottom	¾" x 20" x 34" *	1
(F) Feet	¾" x 3" x 7" (cut to fit)	2

Long point (45 degrees) to long point (45 degrees)

Materials List

Material	Qty
¾" x 4' x 8' AC plywood	1
¼" x 2' x 8' mahogany or bendable plywood	1
1" x 3" x 10' pine	1
1⅛" x 1⅛" x 4' "L" molding	1

How to Build It

Position the plywood good side down, then lay out one crescent-shaped side (A) as shown in Figure 1. Use a jigsaw with a fine-tooth blade to cut ¹⁄₁₆" or so outside the line (cut closer to the line than we show in the photo), then sand up to the line with a belt sander. Trace around this first piece to create the layout for your second side, then cut that side out. *Note*: Layout the plywood so the open crescents face one another; that way you can use the large center "scrap" for the cradle bottom. Next use your router with a rabbeting bit (Photo 3) to cut a ⅜" x ⅜" rabbet around the outside perimeter of your two moon shapes.

Cut the five ribs (B) to length and install them along the edge of the rabbet, using the spacing shown in the diagram. Secure each end of each rib with two trim head drywall screws.

Cut the ¼" plywood for the back (C); we used off-the-shelf lauan plywood (some places call it mahogany) because it's smooth and bends easily. Before installing the back for keeps, we gently "pre-curved" it as shown in Photo 5. We used bar clamps to temporarily hold the back into the rabbets, wetting the backside as we went to relax the fibers. We used wood shims to force the plywood even tighter into the rabbets, then wet it down some more and let it sit overnight.

Four things come in handy when you install the plywood back for real:

1) A helper. One person can bend the plywood into position and install clamps while the other installs shims and fasteners.

2) Slow-setting glue (like Titebond Extend Wood Glue): The extra 10 minutes of open time comes in handy since the process takes a while.

3) A pneumatic or battery powered finish nailer. You want to install lots of nails quickly along the edges to force the plywood tightly into the rabbet.

4) "Flat head" or "washer head" screws. The flat underbelly of these fasteners helps force the plywood against the ribs; "bugle head"

QUICK TIP

If you simply can't get your ¼" plywood to bend without cracking, you can purchase special ¼" bendable plywood from specialty lumber yards. It's more expensive than standard plywood but bends super easily.

drywall screws can drive themselves right through the plywood. If the flat head screws do their job holding the plywood firmly against the glue, you can remove them once the glue sets.

With your helper and materials at the ready, remove the pre-bent plywood, spread the glue into the rabbets and over the first few ribs. Use squeeze clamps and screws to hold one free end of the plywood tight against the first rib then—just as you did during the pre-bending phase—use bar clamps and shims to force the edges of the plywood tightly into the rabbets and against the ribs. *Note:* Let the plywood overhang this first rib by about an inch; you'll trim it later. Use 1" brads to fasten the edges of the plywood (Photo 6) and washer head screws to secure the plywood to the ribs as needed. When you get to the far end, let the excess hang past the last rib and use clamps,

Using It Safely

The feet are positioned to hold the bed of the cradle steady and flat. The cradle is designed so you can rock it forward a little to lull little ones to sleep. But **don't** vigorously rock the cradle past the feet and onto its back. If there's even a remote chance of this happening—due to curious kids, rambunctious dogs, or thick-headed visitors—position the cradle in a corner to prevent a "rollover." An added precaution is to place a sandbag ballast in the bottom (see Photo 10) for stability.

Also make certain that the cradle mattress meets child safety standards. The mattress should fit so two finger widths won't fit between it and the cradle side. Visit the Consumer Product Safety Commission website for more information.

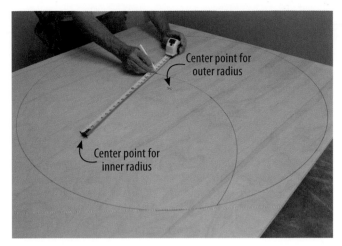

Center point for outer radius

Center point for inner radius

1 **LAY OUT** the crescent-shaped side (A) using a screw for the center point and a tape measure as a large compass.

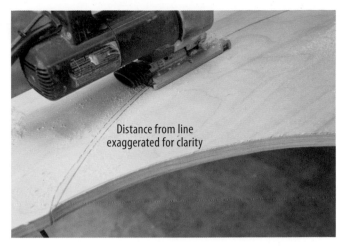

Distance from line exaggerated for clarity

2 **CUT** about ¹⁄₁₆" outside the line (our distance from line exaggerated for clarity) then smooth the edges with a belt sander.

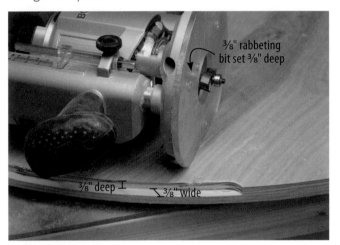

⅜" rabbeting bit set ⅜" deep

⅜" deep

⅜" wide

3 **USE** a router with a ⅜" rabbeting bit to create the groove in the outer edge of the crescent for the plywood back (C).

4 **INSTALL** the five equally-spaced ribs (B) even with the edge of the rabbet. Use bar clamps to temporarily hold the parts together and use trim head screws as fasteners.

nails, screws and glue to hold the plywood end tightly in place (Photo 7). Let the glue set for at least 24 hours before removing the clamps. After you remove the clamps, use a jigsaw to trim the plywood overhanging the end ribs. Install the "L" moldings to "clean up" the edges. Cut the feet and install them as shown Photo 8. If you wish to make decorative cutouts (Photo 9), print out the object, transfer it to the cradle using carbon paper, then cut away. Cut the flat bottom panel (E) from the leftover plywood. Add a sandbag to the bottom for extra stability if you wish (Photo 10), then plop the

bottom in place. Apply your finish of choice. We purchased the die-cut decal quote through Amazon.com. *Lots* of quotes in *lots* of sizes are available.

Watch the Video

Visit spikecarlsen.com to view the video that shows even more tips and tricks for building the Baby-in-the-Moon Cradle.

Perfect Circles with Jigs and Special Bits

Looking to step up your woodworking game? You can create perfect circles and identical sides using a few special jigs and bits.

Begin by cutting out your moon shape leaving ½" or less of material outside the line (Photo 1). Make sure to leave the "tongue" seen in Photo 2; you'll need it as a center point for routing both curves.

The trammel jig (Photo 2) is basically a large compass—made from a router and a ¼" x 4" x 28" scrap of plywood—that can cut plywood circles. To make one, first cut a 1" hole for your router bit a few inches from the end of your ¼" plywood trammel arm. Secure the router base (with the bit chuck centered over the hole) to the plywood with a couple of screws; you may need to remove or add a couple of router base screws to do this. Measure 22" over from the edge of your router bit, make a mark on the far end of your trammel

arm and drill a ⅛" hole. Drive a screw through this hole into the center mark you made when you laid out the plywood side (A) for the outer perimeter. Check and double check to see your bit is positioned so it will cut along your perimeter layout line. When the bit is aligned correctly, rout away the excess plywood to create a perfect outside curve. Mark a new center point on your jig and plywood tongue (Photo 3) for cutting the center curve, then make that cut. Finally use a jigsaw to cut away the remaining base of the tongue.

Now that you have one "perfect" side, you can screw it to a rough-cut blank of the second side and use your router and tracing bit (Photo 4) to create an identical version of the first side.

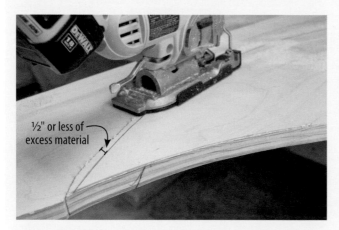

½" or less of excess material

1 **CUT OUT** the crescent moon shape leaving ⅛" to ½" of excess material outside the line. Also, leave material for the "trammel tongue" seen in Photo 13.

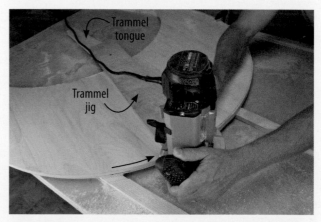

Trammel tongue

Trammel jig

2 **USE** a router with a straight cutting bit and the trammel jig to trim the outer edge of the crescent moon.

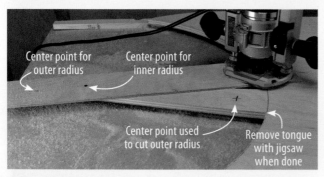

Center point for outer radius

Center point for inner radius

Center point used to cut outer radius

Remove tongue with jigsaw when done

3 **ROUT** the inside edge of the moon. You'll need to move the trammel jig center point closer to the bit and reposition the jig on the tongue to cut the smaller radius. When done, remove the "tongue" with a jigsaw.

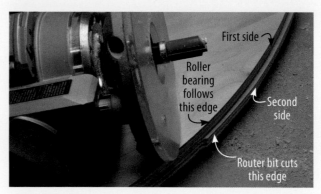

First side

Roller bearing follows this edge

Second side

Router bit cuts this edge

4 **CUT** the second crescent moon side using the first side as a template and a tracing bit to do the cutting.

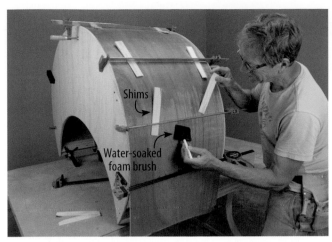

5 **PRE-BEND** the plywood by gently coaxing it into a curve with bar clamps and shims. Wet the backside as you go to help "relax" the wood fibers. Let this sit overnight.

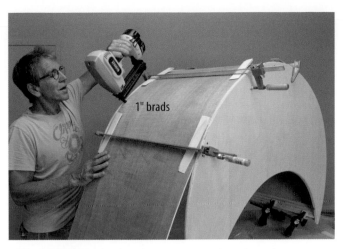

6 **INSTALL** the back permanently using slow-setting glue, 1" brads, washer head screws, clamps and—if possible—a helper.

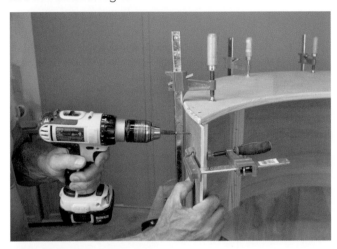

7 **SECURE** the ends—the areas under the greatest tension— with washer head screws. Let the glue cure for 24 hours before removing clamps.

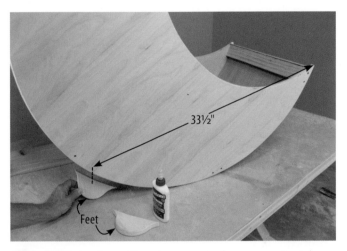

8 **ADD** the feet. Cut them out of scrap material and position them based on the measurements in the diagram.

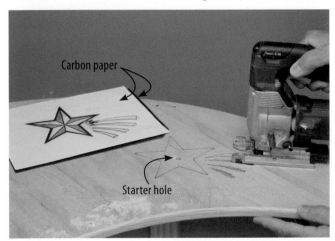

9 **TRANSFER** whatever shapes you like onto the plywood using carbon paper, then cut carefully with a fine-tooth jigsaw blade.

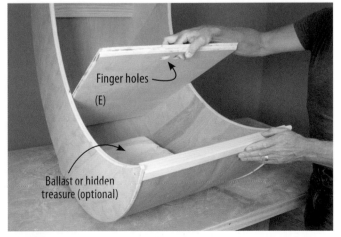

10 **SET** the bottom (E) in place. Use the storage area beneath for ballast for stability or to hide stuff.

Lumber Lingo 101

Most of the lumber and plywood in this book is "off the shelf" material purchased from the big box store down the block. As you stroll down Lumber Lane at your outlet, here's some lingo to help you pick the right stuff.

Nominal vs. Actual Dimensions

"Nominal" is the "lumberyard name" for boards and their dimensions. **"Actual"** refers to, well, the actual dimensions of a board. In this book, we list *nominal* dimensions in the materials lists and *actual* dimensions in the parts and cutting lists. This way, when you go shopping you can say "Two 1x4s please," but while you're building, it computes that those two boards laid side-by-side add up to 7 inches.

Photos **A** and **B** show the nominal and actual dimensions of common lumberyard material.

Grade

When you're buying boards, you'll usually encounter two or three "grades." In general, the fewer the knots and "cleaner" the edges, the higher the grade (and lower the number).

Construction grade, standard or #3 boards are inexpensive but contain a wide range of defects. If you're tackling a project with lots of short pieces, you can save money buying this grade and cutting out the defects—but long twisted, bowed and cupped boards can be a hassle to work with.

Quality or #2 boards may have small, tight knots and other defects but are fine for most projects—especially those that get painted.

Premium, select or #1 boards should be straight and knot free with nice square edges. Premium lumber costs three of four times that of construction grade lumber, but it behaves better. (**Photo C**)

Species

There are around 80,000 species of wood on the planet—but you'll most likely find only three or four at your local lumberyard. The most common include:

Pine is widely available, reasonably priced, relatively stable and easy to work.

Oak is the most commonly stocked hardwood in home centers. It's moderately priced, tough as nails and straight grained. Take your time picking through the stack when buying oak boards—if your project requires two or more boards, you'll want them to match in color and grain.

Maple is commonly stocked, has a nice light color, has a hardness somewhere between that of pine and oak and sports a grain that doesn't call attention to itself—even though, you'll sometimes discover a gem. Its' smooth surface paints like a dream. (**Photo D**)

Plywood

Most plywood, whether it's construction plywood or maple hardwood, usually has two letters—ranging from A to D—in its description. Each letter relates to the quality of one of the faces. A sheet labeled AB has one top-notch side and one "pretty good" side. A sheet labeled CDX means neither side looks all that great (the "X" means its rated for outdoor use.)

Also, pay attention to the composition of the core. Most contain an odd-number of plies—the more the better. Sheets with particle board cores are usually cheaper but have lousy nail- and screw holding ability. Those with lumber cores are expensive but can be glued, screwed and nailed like regular lumber. (**Photo E**)

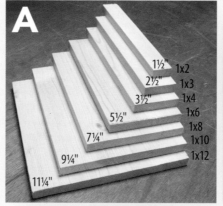

A

1½" 1x2
2½" 1x3
3½" 1x4
5½" 1x6
 1x8
7¼" 1x10
9¼" 1x12
11¼"

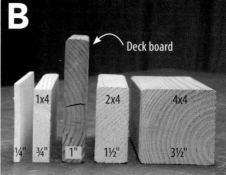

B

Deck board

1x4   2x4   4x4

¼" ¾" 1" 1½" 3½"

C

D

E

Bedroom Step & Stool

Some people call this a Franklin stool, others a flip stool. I call it the super-duper handy bedroom stool. Sure, it's handy in bathrooms for getting "sink high" for brushing teeth and washing hands. And in kitchens it provides that height boost kids often need. But in bedrooms, kids can use it for getting into bed, reaching high-hanging stuff in closets or for just sitting around. We made ours from oak, but pine or other woods will work just as well.

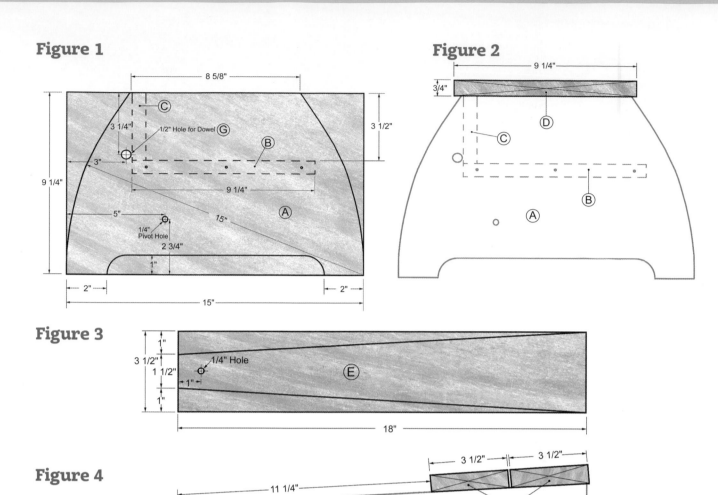

Figure 1

Figure 2

Figure 3

Figure 4

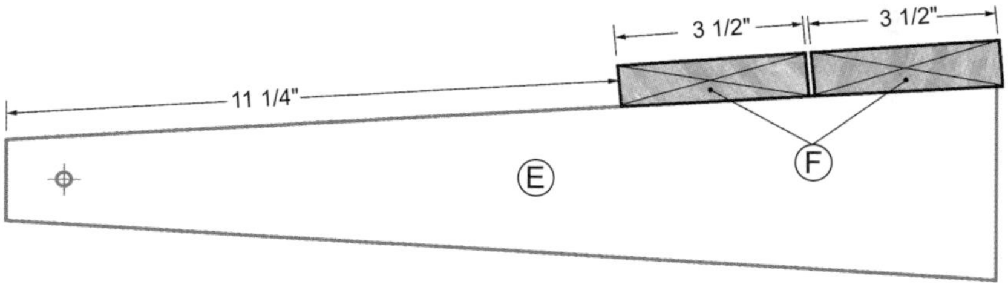

How to Build It

Cut the two side panels (A) to length. Use the lower corners as center points and draw the curved sides using a tape measure and pencil (Photo 1). The sides panels are mirror images; mark one LEFT and one RIGHT so you don't screw up. Mark the positions for the pivot holes and stop dowels (G) too. Use a quarter to mark the radii for the lower leg cutouts.

Cut the side panels to shape (Photo 2). Cut just outside the line, then finish by sanding up to the line with a power sander. Soften the edges with a ¼" round-over bit (Photo 3). Use this same bit to soften the edges of other parts later on, too.

Cutting List

Part	Dimensions	Qty
(A) Sides	¾" x 9¼" x 15"	2
(B) Shelf	¾" x 9¼" x 13¼"	1
(C) Back panel	¾" x 3½" x 13¼"	1
(D) Seat	¾" x 9¼" x 14¾"	1
(E) Swing arm	¾" x 3½" x 18	2
(F) Slats	¾" x 3½" x 16½"	2
(G) Stop dowel	½" x 1"	2

Materials List

Part	Qty	
1 x 10 x 6'	1	*Note: All materials are oak*
1 x 4 x 8'	1	
½" dowel	short piece	
½" oak plugs	20	

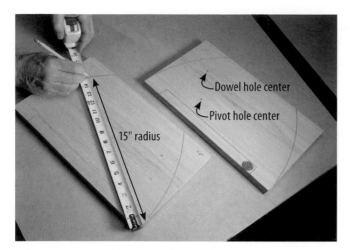

1 **LAY OUT** the two side panels as shown in Diagram A, including center points for the swing down step assembly and the stop peg.

2 **CUT OUT** the sides using a jigsaw. Cut just outside the line, then use a power sander to sand right up to the line.

3 **USE** a router to soften the outside edges of the side panels. You'll use the same bit to soften the edges of the back and leg assembly parts, too.

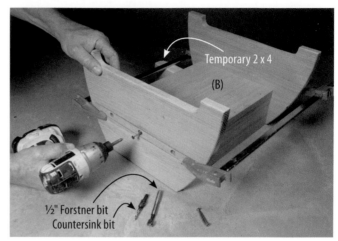

4 **SECURE** the 1x4 back panel (C) to the shelf (B) to create an "L," then screw both to the side panels. The 2x4s in the background position the shelf at the right height.

Secure the back panel (C) to the shelf (B) using glue and 6d finish nails, then secure this L-shape to the side panels (Photo 4). Use a scrap 2x4 (seen in the background) to prop up the seat so the seat is positioned flat and at the right height. To create holes for the plugs and the fasteners, first drill the ¼" deep x ½" diameter holes for the plugs, then bore the countersink holes for the screws themselves.

Install the seat (D) using glue and screws. Glue the stop dowel (G) in place as shown in Photo 5. Taper cut the swing arms (E) as

shown in Figures 3 and 4 then secure the two footrest/back boards (F) to them making sure the distance between the arms is 15" to allow clearance for the arms to swing freely. Bore the pivot holes in the arms and side panels. Tape a washer over the pivot hole as shown in Photo 5, slide the bolt through the arm and the sides, then secure using another washer and a bolt.

Stop dowel

Washer taped in place

2" bolt

(F)

½" plugs

5 **SCREW** the slats (F) to the wide ends of the swing arms (E). Bore pivot holes in the arms and side panels. Tape washers over the side panel pivot holes, position the leg assembly, then secure with a bolt, nut and washer.

6 **SAND** and finish. Glue wood plugs into the holes—leaving them proud about ¹⁄₁₆"—then sand smooth. Stain and apply a clear finish of your choice.

Glue the plugs in place, leaving the heads about ¹⁄₁₆" proud of (above) the surface. Use a random orbital sander (Photo 6) to flatten the plugs and remove dried glue, then use an eraser to remove remaining pencil marks. Sand all the surfaces with progressively fine sandpaper, then apply the stain and clear finish of choice.

QUICK TIP

If you don't want to go through the extra work of installing the decorative plugs, simply install trim head screws and apply colored putty over the screw holes during finishing.

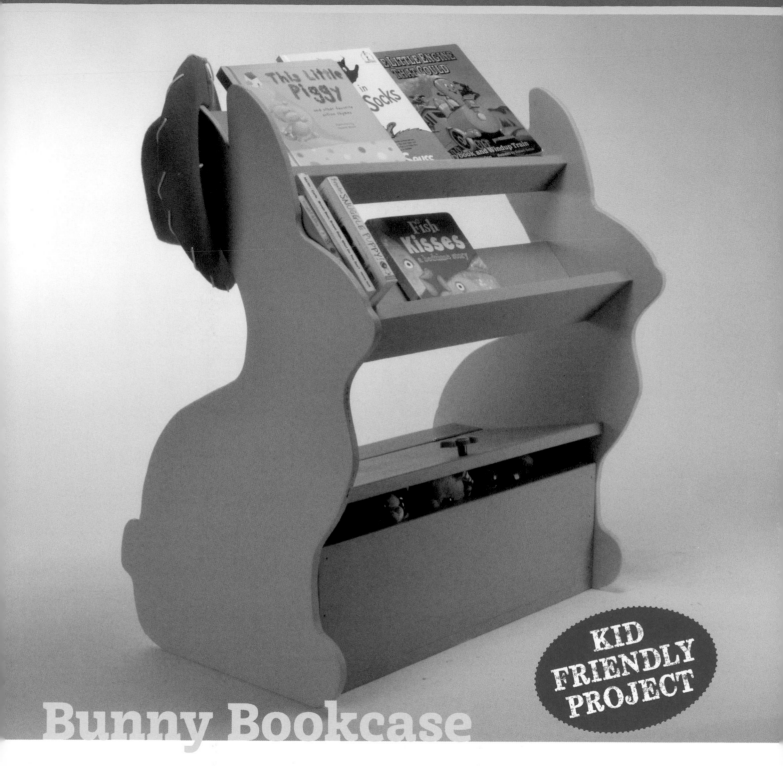

Bunny Bookcase

A good project for kids to hop into

Most kids have way more stuff than they know what to do with. This project provides storage space for at least 2% of that stuff. It may not be big, but it makes up for that in cute. The chest provides a great place for stashing stuffed animals, and the shelves are ideal for storing and displaying books and pictures (or *more* stuffed animals). Still not enough space? Build an entire warren of these bunny bookcases (they won't reproduce on their own).

How to Build It

Enlarge the pattern on a copy machine until the bunny is 30½" tall. This will eventually involve taping 9 standard sheets of paper together to create the final life size pattern. The Rocking Pony project (p. 111) has more information on this process.

Use carbon paper to transfer the bunny outline and shelf positions onto the plywood. Use a jigsaw to cut out this first side then sand the edges smooth (Photo 1). Use this as a pattern to draw the second side. Use a router with a round over bit or sandpaper to ease the edges.

Next build the chest. All the boards (with the exception of the sides) are 24-in. long and none require ripping. Secure the front and back (D) to the sides (C), then nail this to the bottom (B). Glue and nail the lid hinge brace (E) to the backside of the box, then install the hinges and lid (Photo 2).

Use clamps to hold the bunny sides against the chest (Photo 3) then check how everything fits. The front of the chest should sit just behind the front of the bunny's legs. Once you're satisfied with the fit, remove the clamps, apply glue to the sides of the chest then clamp the sides back in place. Open the lid and drive a few 1" drywall screws through the chest and into the plywood sides.

Build the "V"s that form the lower (G,H) and upper (J,K) slanted shelves. Note the directions

Figure 1

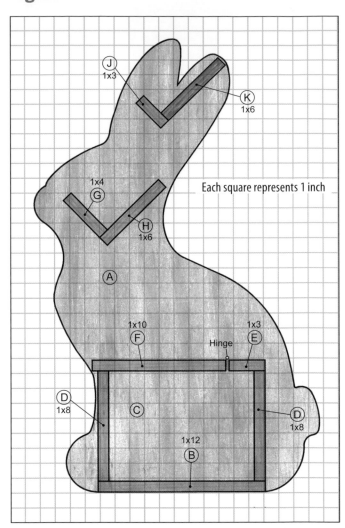

Each square represents 1 inch

Cutting List

Part	Dimensions	Qty
(A) Side	½" x 20" x 30" plywood	2
(B) Chest bottom	¾" x 11¼" x 24"	1
(C) Chest sides	¾" x 7¼" x 9¾"	2
(D) Chest front & back	¾" x 7¼" x 24	2
(E) Lid hinge brace	¾" x 2½" x 24"	1
(F) Chest Lid	¾" x 9¼" x 24"	1
(G) Lower shelf front	¾" x 3½" x 24"	1
(H) Lower shelf back	¾" x 5½" x 24"	1
(J) Upper shelf front	¾" x 2½" x 24"	1
(K) Upper shelf back	¾" x 5½" x 24"	1

Materials List

Material	Qty
½" x 20" x 60" AC plywood	1
1 x 12 x 2'	1
1 x 10 x 2'	1
1 x 8 x 4'	2
1 x 6 x 4'	1
1 x 4 x 2'	1
1 x 3 x 4'	1

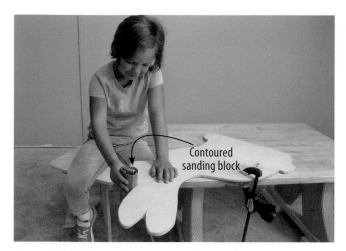

1 **CREATE** the bunny sides (A). Enlarge the pattern, then use carbon paper to transfer the shape to the plywood for the first side. Cut out the shape, sand the edges smooth then use this as a template for the second side.

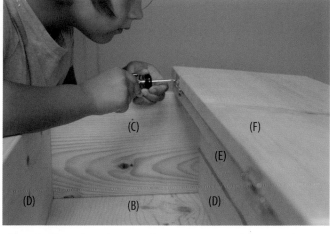

2 **BUILD** the chest. All parts are 24" long and made from standard width boards. Install the hinge as the last step of the process.

3 **APPLY** glue to the sides of the chest, then use clamps to secure the bunny panels on each side. Add a few drywall screws, driven from inside the chest, for added strength.

4 **BUILD** the shelf "V"s, then use clamps to hold them in position while driving the trim head screws. A helper—especially a smiley one—comes in handy here.

the edges of the boards butt together so you don't wind up with a shelf that doesn't fit. Since you laid out the positions of shelves on the insides of the side panels, you have great guides for predrilling the holes for the screws that will hold the shelves in place. Bore the holes from the inside (where the shelves are marked.) When you install the shelves (Photo 4) drive the screws from the outside into the ends of the shelves.

Paint your bunny "hutch" as you see fit, then load it up.

QUICK TIP

I built this alongside my seven-year-old granddaughter, Morgan. We took turns. She transferred the pattern onto the plywood; I cut it out. She sanded some edges; I routed some edges. She measured and marked the boards to length—all but two of the boards are 24" long for ease—and I cut them. Well you get the idea. You'll develop your own "work flow" as you work with kids. Just remember to take your time, be safe and have fun.

Cheery Cherry Toy Chest

A challenging classic that will last a lifetime

We call this a toy chest—but it's a book case, a knickknack box and a fun place to sit and read. And when your kids are grown, it makes one heck of a fine entry bench.

This is one of the more challenging projects in the book. It involves biscuit joints, sunken panels and cutting tight curves. Plus, it's made from cherry—a mistake in this material costs three times as much as a mistake in pine! So, if you're a beginner, consider sharpening your chops on a couple of other projects before digging into this one.

We show two versions of the finished chest. One with cherry plywood panels; another with panels

Top

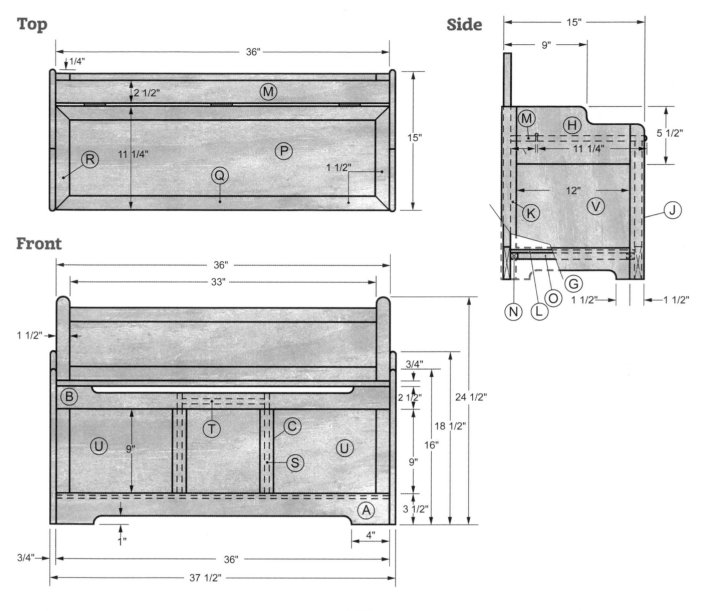

Side

Front

Back

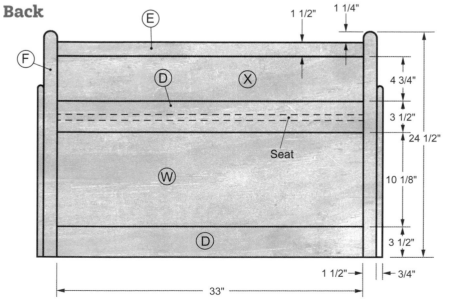

Seat

Materials List

Material	Qty
¾" x ¾" x 8' cherry	1
1 x 2 x 8' cherry	3
1 x 3 x 8' cherry	1
1 x 4 x 8' cherry	1
1 x 6 x 4' cherry	1
¼" x ¾" x 8' cherry	1
¼" x 4' x 8' cherry plywood	1
¾" x 4' x 8' cherry plywood	1
1½" hinges	3
Soft close hinge	1

painted by children's book author, Nancy Carlson (find out more at nancycarlson.com). We encourage you to have fun decorating your flat panels in your own unique way.

How to Build It

The main chest consists of four frames. Building them takes a fair amount of work, skill and focus, but once they're constructed you're over halfway home. All the parts are made from standard width lumber, so you won't have any ripping to do. We used cherry, but any softwood or hardwood will work just as well.

Cutting List

Part	Dimension	Qty
A) Front bottom rail	¾" x 3½" x 36"	1
B) Front top rail	¾" x 2½" x 36"	1
C) Front stile	¾" x 1½" x 9"	4
D) Back bottom & mid rail	¾" x 3½" x 33"	2
E) Back top rail	¾" x 1½" x 33"	1
F) Back side stile	¾" x 1½" x 24½"	2
G) Side bottom rail	¾" x 3½" x 12"	2
H) Side top rail	¾" x 5½" x 12"	2
I) Note: To avoid confusion, no "I"s included in parts lists		
J) Side front stile	¾" x 1½" x 16"	2
K) Side back stile	¾" x 1½" x 18½"	2
L) Chest bottom	¼" x 13" x 36" plywood	1
M) Top lid support	¾" x 2½" x 36"	1
N) Long bottom support	¾" x ¾" x 36"	2
O) Short bottom support	¾" x ¾" x 11½"	2
P) Lid center core	¾" x 8¼" x 32⅞" plywood	1
Q) Lid long frame member	¾" x 1½" x 35⅞" *	2
R) Lid short frame member	¾" x 1½" x 11¼" *	2
S) Inner divider verticals	¾" x 13" x 11½" plywood **	2
T) Inner divider top	¾" x 13" x 8½" plywood	1
U) Front panel	¼" x 9¾" x 11⅝" plywood	2
V) Side panel	¼" x 10¼" x 12⅝" plywood	2
W) Back panel	¼" x 10⅝" x 33⅝" plywood	1
X) Back rest panel	¼" x 5½" x 33⅝" plywood	1

*Indicates long point to long point
**Cut to fit

Begin by using a miter saw to cut parts A through K to length. Make the curved cuts on the bottoms of parts A and G, as well as the rounded armrests on part H. Build the four frames (Photo 1) using glue, biscuits and clamps (for additional information on biscuit joiner basics, see "Riley's Rocking Chair" and visit YouTube.) Use a router with a ⅜" rabbeting bit (Photo 2) to cut the ¼" deep rabbets on the insides of the frame openings (except for the middle opening of the front panel.) These recesses hold the flat panels installed in Photo 8.

Next mark the locations of the biscuits used to join the frames to one another. Use clamps to temporarily hold the parts in position (Photo 3) and mark the centers of the biscuits. Note the front and back panels are inset ¼" in from the ends of the side panels; use a scrap piece of ¼" plywood to establish that inset. Cut the slots as shown in Photo 4. Adjust the biscuit joiner fence to cut the center of the slot ⅜ inch back from the "inset" line. Test fit your frames as shown in Photo 5. If everything aligns, apply glue to the biscuits, slots and edges of the frame and clamp them together.

Glue and screw the lid support (M) to the back of the chest (Photo 6.) Install the bottom supports (N,O), then use glue and brads to secure the bottom (L) in place as shown in Photo 7.

Cut the flat panels (U, V, W, X) to size, then round the corners as seen in Photo 8. Use glue and ½" brads to secure the panels into the openings. Install the vertical dividers (S), divider top (T) and trim pieces as seen in Photo 9. (Note, the flat panels have been removed for clarity.)

Build the lid (Photo 10.) Use biscuits to secure the perimeter pieces (Q, R) to the plywood core (P) and to one another at the corners. Install the hinges and lid support (Photo 11.) Apply your finish of choice then step back and admire your work—and the joy this toy chest brings.

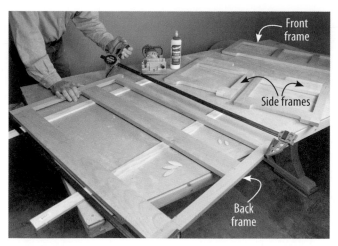

1 **BUILD** the front, back and side frames using glue and biscuits for joinery. These four frames create the main structure of the chest.

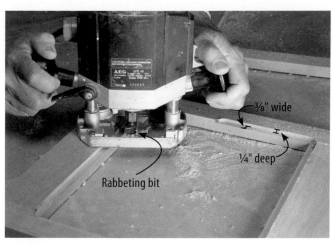

2 **ROUT** ¼" deep recesses in the backs of the frames to receive the flat panels, using a router and a ⅜" rabbeting bit.

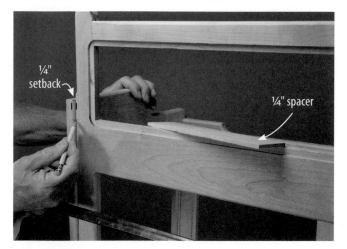

3 **MARK** the locations of the centers of the biscuits on the panels. The ¼" plywood in the foreground is used to establish the side panel setback shown.

4 **CUT** slots in the side pieces for joining the front and back panels. Again account for the ¼" setback when cutting your slots.

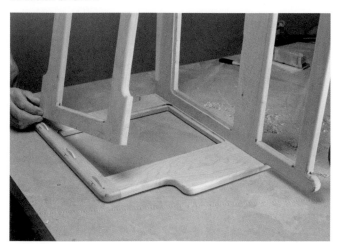

5 **TEST FIT** the panels, then secure them to one another using biscuits and glue. Use lots of clamps; you shouldn't have to use nails or screws.

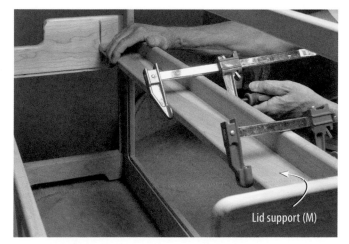

6 **GLUE** and clamp the lid support (M) to the back panel. Secure the ends to the side panels with 6d finish nails.

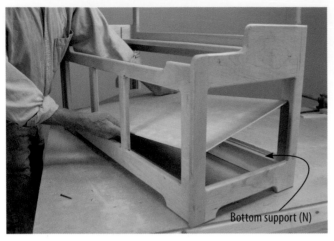

7 **INSTALL** the bottom, securing it to the ¾" x ¾" bottom supports with glue and ½" brads.

Bottom support (N)

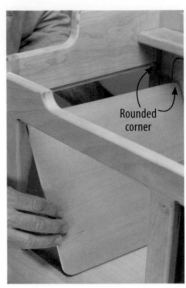

Rounded corner

8 **TEST FIT** the inset panels. Fine tune the size as needed, then secure them into the opening with glue and ½" brads.

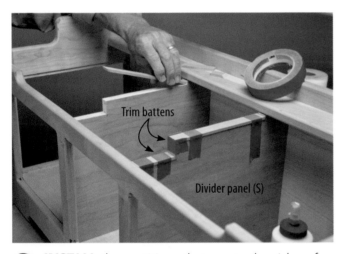

Trim battens

Divider panel (S)

9 **INSTALL** the partitions that create the sides of the bookcase area. Tape the ¼" cherry battens in place, then secure the tray to the partitions (T) with finish nails.

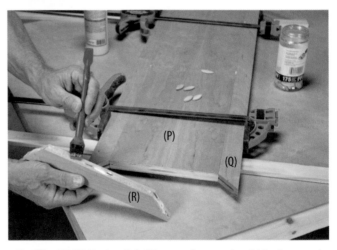

(P)

(Q)

(R)

10 **BUILD** the lid. Picture frame the ¾" plywood with strips of solid cherry wood, using glue and biscuits.

The Right Finish for Cherry

The easiest finish to apply is a rub-on poly or Danish Oil. But solid wood, ¼" plywood and ¾" plywood each accept finish slightly differently. If you want to create a more uniform look you can make "story boards" using scrap pieces of lumber and plywood. These allow you to compare finishes and how they look on various types of materials. This can all be complicated by the fact that cherry naturally darkens when exposed to sunlight. We wound up applying sanding sealer, followed by two coats of Cherry Danish Oil.

11 **SCREW** the hinges and closer mechanism to the lid and chest. The closer has slow moving spring action to help protect little fingers.

Workshop Safety

I've been working around saws, drills and other power tools for 45 years—and still have 10 fingers, 2 eyes and 0 visits to the emergency room. (My hearing's another story.) I'd like to think this safety record is due to common sense, eternal vigilance and learning from the few close calls I've had.

Unplugging power tools when changing bits, blades or belts is a must. And supporting sheets of plywood and boards with scrap lumber—so the two halves don't pinch the blade, causing the saw to kickback as you cut—will also eliminate a common cause of accidents.

Keep your hands out of harm's way. When using utility knives, chisels, screwdrivers and other sharp tools, ask yourself, "What's going to happen if this tool suddenly slips or skips?" Then rearrange your body parts accordingly. (**Photo A**)

Clamp stuff down. It only takes one hit below the belt to learn clamping boards down when using large drill bits is a very good idea. But clamps are a fabulous "third hand" in lots of circumstances. Use them when sawing short boards or to wiggle-proof two boards while fastening them to one another or for holding one end of a long board while you're installing the other. (**Photo B**)

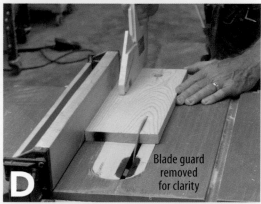

Wear hearing and eye protection. When I was young and invincible I never wore hearing protectors; now I'm paying the price by saying "Huh?" 50 times a day. Now I wear my hearing protectors "Mickey Mouse" style on top of my head and slip them on before clicking on any power tool and even before using some hand tools. Wear safety glasses when circumstances dictate. (**Photo C**)

Use push sticks, push blocks and feather boards when using stationary power tools; you'll get more accurate results and keep your fingers out of harm's way. (**Photo D**)

Blade guard removed for clarity

Remember, fasteners can fasten you. Keep fingers out of the path of any fasteners you're driving—especially if you're using pneumatic or cordless nailers. It only takes a fraction of a second to "fasten" yourself. (**Photo E**)

Circus Train for Stuffies

Hook 'em together for play; stack 'em up for storage

In 1880, a German Company named Steiff became the first commercial company to create a stuffed toy—and kids have been cuddling them and collecting them ever since. If the kids in your life are like most, they have a lot of toys to cuddle—and stow.

These circus train cars are storage boxes in disguise. They can be used in two modes: Hooked together for play and stacked atop one another for storage. The bungee cord bars stretch to make it easy to slide toys in and out when playing or when the cars are stacked. It's a great project to do hand-in-hand with kids.

How to Build It

Cut the top (A) and bottom (B) boards to length. Use a hole saw to drill four 3½" holes in the corners of the opening in the top board, then finish cutting the opening with a jigsaw. Hang onto the circular cut outs—they're soon to become circus car wheels. (*Note:* Don't let kids use a hole saw; hole saws can be hard to control, and can jerk the entire drill

Top View

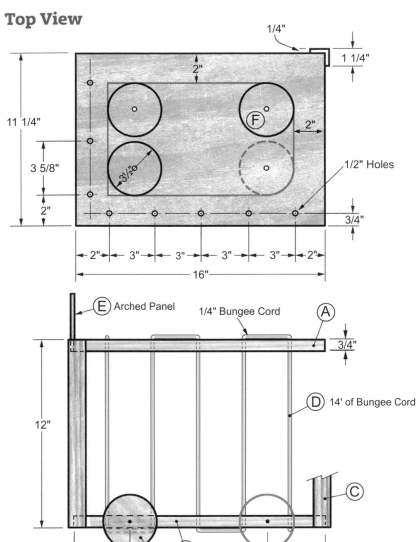

Dimension labels

(Top View diagram labels: 1/4", 1 1/4", 2", 11 1/4", 3 5/8", 2", 3½", 2", 1/2" Holes, 3/4", 2" — 3" — 3" — 3" — 3" — 2", 16", F)

Cutting List (per car)

Part	Dimensions	Qty
(A) Top	1" x 12" x 16"	1
(B) Bottom	1" x 12" x 16"	1
(C) Corners	1⅛" x 1⅛" x 12"	4
(D) Bungee bars	¼" bungee cord	12'
(E) Arched top panel	¼" x 3" x 9"	2
(F) Wheels	3½" diameter (approx.)	4

Materials List (per car)

Material	Qty
1" x 12" x 3' pine	1
¼" x 1⅛" x 4' corner molding	1
¼" x 4" x 2' pine	1
¼" bungee cord *	12'

* Purchased through Amazon

(Front View diagram labels: E Arched Panel, 1/4" Bungee Cord, A, 3/4", D 14' of Bungee Cord, 12", C, B, F, 3 1/2", 3 1/2")

Arched Top Panel

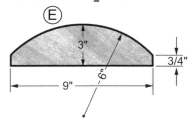

(Arched Top Panel diagram labels: E, 3", 6", 3/4", 9")

Front View

if they catch on an edge). Use a ½" drill bit (Photo 1) to bore the bungee cord holes.

Cut the four corner supports (C) to length (Photo 2). Position the corner supports between the top and bottom, then secure with glue and 3d finish nails (Photo 3). Predrill holes to prevent splitting.

Once the glue has dried, weave the bungee cord (D) though the holes. Start by securing one loose end of the cord to one corner of the bottom with a horseshoe fence staple. After you weave a side, go back and re-stretch the cords, taking up slack as you go. The

tension is about right when you can bend a "bar" and it just touches its neighbor. Once all the bars are woven and tensioned right, secure the free end of the bungee cord with another fence staple and trim off the excess.

Install the wheels (Photo 5.) First, drill the axle holes in the bottom (B) then slide a washer, a wheel and another washer (in that order) over the shank of a 2-in screw. Install and tighten that screw in the axle hole. Finally, glue and nail the upper arched end panels (E) between the corner supports.

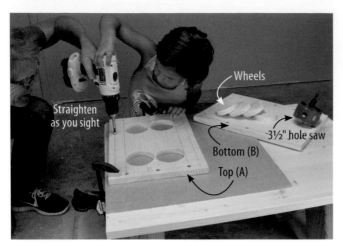

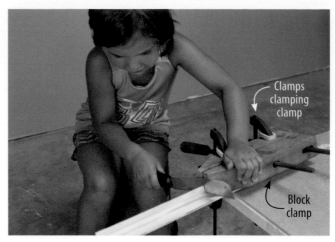

1 **PREPARE** the top (A) and bottom (B) panels. Bore holes for the bungee cord through both panels. The four circles drilled for the corner opening become the wheels (seen in background).

2 **CUT** the corner supports. The block clamp holds the molding steady, establishes the right length and provides a square surface for the saw to ride against—all things that make cutting easier for kids.

3 **SECURE** the corner supports (C) using glue and 3d finish nails. Predrill holes to prevent splitting.

4 **WEAVE** the bungee cord through the holes. After finishing a side, go back and pull the cord tighter to take up the slack, then continue on.

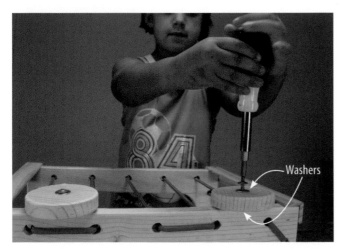

5 **SCREW** the wheels to the bottom. Predrill axle holes and include a washer between the wheel and the bottom so wheels will freely turn.

QUICK TIPS

To get straight, vertical holes use the "two-person drill press method." The drillers position themselves 90-degrees from each other and grab the drill handle. Each person sights the bit from their angle and straightens the drill accordingly.

It's a whole lot easier to paint the circus car and the wheels before installing the bungee cord and wheels.

Crazy Cube Shelf & Hooks

A colorful bedroom organizer from scrap

If you've been building projects from this book, chances are you have a nicely stocked scrap bin by now. If you've made mistakes, it may be *really* full. Here's a project that'll put those cutoffs—and some hammer happy kid—to work. This "Crazy Cube Shelf" is anything goes—we don't include dimensions or materials lists since half the fun (maybe even ¾ of the fun) is building something to suit your kids' space, needs, and stuff (and your scrap pile.)

1 **PREDRILL** holes for 6d finish nails. Clamps are a great way to hold parts together and keep them square while nailing.

2 **NAIL** the corners together. Kids should wear safety glasses when driving nails; add hearing protectors when things get noisy.

3 **APPLY** dabs of hot melt glue to the backs of the boxes, then push them into place. Later, go back and secure them permanently with screws.

4 **INSTALL** the pegs. Drill the ½" holes, then use glue to secure the pre-painted pegs in place. Secure your new creation to the wall.

How to Build It

Dig through your scrap bin for "one by" (1x3, 1x4, 1x8, etc.) cutoffs; any width, length and species is fair game. Determine what size boxes you want—or have enough material for—and cut the sides to length. Our smallest box required 12" of material; our largest about 36". Secure three sides with a clamp as shown in Photo 1, predrill holes, then nail them together using two or three 6d nails per joint (Photo 2). Add the fourth side.

Paint the boxes (a great use for leftover paint!) Experiment with the positions of your boxes and pegs, then cut a piece of plywood—one at least ½" thick—to size. Mark the positions of your boxes and pegs on the plywood, then use hot melt glue (Photo 3) to temporarily secure the boxes to the plywood. After all the boxes are installed, go back and secure the backs of the boxes with screws driven in through the plywood.

Mark the locations of the clothes pegs, drill holes, then secure them in place with wood glue (Photo 4). Locate two or more wall studs—once you find the first one, the others are usually 16" away—then use drywall screws to secure the rack to the wall.

Buildin' with Children

This book is about building furniture for kids, but it can be extremely gratifying—for all parties—to build projects with kids. There are lots of great reasons to work side-by-side with little people:

It's a gateway to other kinds of learning. Build a catapult with a kid and they're also learning physics (so THAT's how levers work), math (this plus this equals THAT), scientific research (adjusting the counterweight does THAT), history (Alexander the Great did THAT with them?) and more.

It fosters creativity. I recently built mangers with 90 fourth graders. They all started out with the same four boards for the walls—but in the end every single one wound up different.

Learning how to use tools is a skill kids will use for a lifetime.

It's a great way to spend time together—and there's something special about an activity where you walk away with a physical object.

When you build stuff with kids, follow the same code of ethics doctors adhere to: DO NO HARM. Work slowly, thoughtfully and one-on-one. Start with the basics: Hammering, measuring, clamping, painting and gluing—then work your way up to other tools.

Clamp stuff down so kids can focus on the tool—not holding stuff still. Clamps also allow kids to keep both hands on the tool, and can, like above, provide a guide for sawing boards squarely and to the right length.

Provide a kid-height workbench so they don't have to work on the floor or teetering on a stool. It doesn't have to be fancy—an old door perched on a pair of sawed off sawhorses works great.

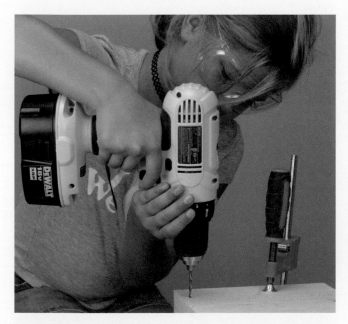

Protect eyes and ears with safety goggles and hearing protectors when needed. And YOU should provide a good example by doing the same.

Predrill holes for screws and nails. One of the keys to fostering the DIY spirit in kids is to minimize frustration. Bent nails, smashed thumbs and split boards can all be avoided by creating a pathway to glory for the fasteners.

Cube-Iture

Simple, clever modular furniture—for life

Here's modular furniture you can use from the day you change your kid's first diaper 'til the day you attend their college graduation—and beyond. We call it *Cube-Iture*, but it's really just a collection of plywood cubes and triangles you can stack together in dozens of creative and useful ways.

They're each exactly 15¾" x 15¾" x 15¾", which means you can stack them side-by-side, side-by-back, upside down or backwards and they'll fit together as precisely as kids' building blocks. It also means they make insanely good use of a sheet of plywood; there's almost no waste.

We built 14 units: Four open cubes, four drawer cubes, two door cubes and four triangular half cubes. You can build more or fewer depending on your needs.

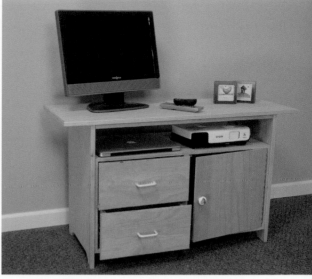

Use plywood and store-bought feet to create dozens of configurations. Clockwise, from upper left: **Eating Nook** (bun feet and 18"x 42" plywood for table; casters, 1x4s and 18"x 18" plywood for chair). **Entertainment Center** (16"x 28" plywood sides, 18"x 40" plywood top). **Playhouse Dresser** (bun feet). **Reading Nook** (1x4 raised base). **Desk** (18"x 48" plywood top, 4/4 x 3" risers).

Cutting List for Basic Cube

Part	Dimensions	Qty
(A) Side	½" x 15¾" (length) x 15½" (width)	2
(B) Top, bottom, and middle partitions	½" x 15¼" (length) x 15½" (width)	2*
(C) Back	¼" x 15¾" x 15¾"	1

* 3 are needed for drawer units

Figure 1

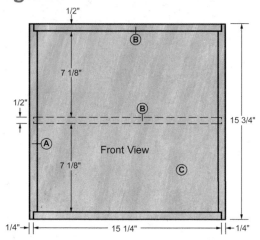

Front View

1/2"
7 1/8"
1/2"
15 3/4"
7 1/8"
1/4" — 15 1/4" — 1/4"

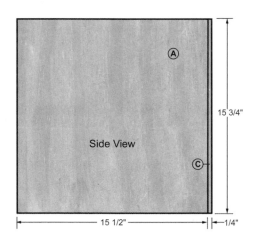

Side View

15 3/4"
15 1/2" — 1/4"

Build the Basic Cube

You need to turn big 4' x 8' rectangles of plywood into lots of smaller ones. Hands down, the fastest, most accurate way to do this is with a table saw. You *can* use a circular saw and straight cutting jig (see page 104) but it's gonna take a lot longer and you'll need to be absolutely meticulous (entirely possible) for your pieces to be uniform. A table saw (Photo 2) comes in handy for cutting the rabbets and dados in the plywood anyway (though there ARE other ways of handling this, too) so we suggest you beg, borrow, buy or rent a table saw for this project.

Determine how many cubes you're going to make; you can get enough side, top and bottom panels from each sheet of plywood to build 4½ basic cubes. We used ½" A-C plywood with one relatively smooth, knot-free face and the other with some knots, but no large flaws—and painted them. If you want a natural wood look, use hardwood plywood like birch, Apple ply or oak. If you want to save money you can use a lower grade construction plywood or even particleboard.

Rip the plywood into 15½" wide strips as shown in Photo 1. Next, cut these strips to the length; half (A) will be 15¾" long and half (B) will be 15¼" long. If you cut these to length on a table saw employ a side extension table or

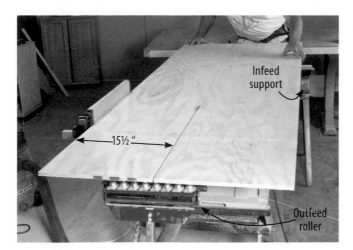

1 **CUT** the plywood to width and length. (In this photo, one 15 ½" wide strip has already been cut.) Use out-feed rollers, out-feed tables or a helper to handle the big sheets safely.

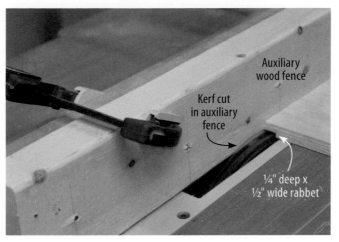

2 **USE** a dado blade to cut ¼" deep by ½" wide rabbets on both ends of the side pieces (A). Use a wood auxiliary fence with a kerfed cutout as shown for best results.

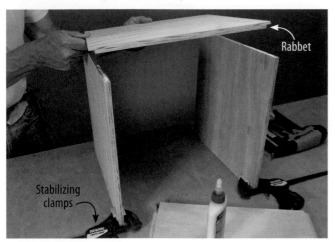

3 **ASSEMBLE** the cubes using wood glue and nails. We used a pneumatic finish nailer, but you can do it the good old fashioned way—with a hammer and nails.

4 **INSTALL** the ¼" back as soon as you've built a cube. The back will help "square up" the cube and add rigidity.

rollers to help support the uncut portion of the plywood as you work. The strips become less awkward to maneuver as they become shorter. You can also cut strips to length with the proverbial circular saw and straight cutting jig.

Next, use a dado blade to cut rabbets on both ends of the side panels (A). Install a ⅝" (or wider) dado blade and an auxiliary wood fence (Photo 2). Lower the blade below the saw surface, adjust the fence so the outer edge of the dado blade is ½" away, then slowly raise the blade—cutting into the edge of the

wood fence. Adjust the blade to a ¼" height. Run ½" plywood scraps along the fence and adjust the fence and blade until you create

> **QUICK TIP**
>
> *A "rabbeted" joint is stronger than a "butt" joint—but you can forget all this rabbeting stuff and use simple butt joints. Just make sure to adjust the lengths of pieces A and B so you wind up with truly cubical cubes.*

a dado exactly ½" wide, ¼" deep. Then cut dados along both ends of the side panels.

Assemble the cubes as shown in Photo 3. *Note:* If you're making drawer units cut the center dado (see Photo 7) before assembling the cubes. You can use 4d finish nails and a hammer to assemble the boxes but, again, a certain power tool—in this case, a pneumatic or cordless nailer—can save you tons of time. Once the cube is built, immediately install the ¼" plywood back to "square up" the cube and add rigidity as the glue sets (Photo 4).

Okay, you've built your basic cubes. The following sections show you how to build the drawer, door and triangular units

Build the Door Units

Cut the door panel to size; it should be ⅛" smaller in width and length than the opening. Install a 12" long piano hinge along one edge of the door, then secure it to the cube as shown in Photo 5.

Install a knob or handle and add the little stop blocks shown in Photo 6 to prevent the door from swinging in too far. You can also add a magnetic catch to ensure the door remains shut.

Watch the Video
Visit spikecarlsen.com to see the video that shows even more tips and tricks for building cube-iture.

Cutting List for Door

Part	Dimensions	Qty
(H) Door	½" x 14⅝" x 14⅝"	1

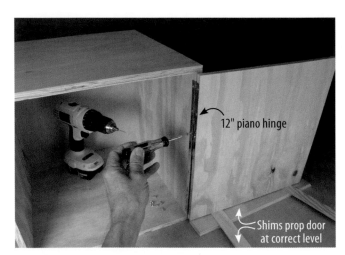

5 **SECURE** one leg of the piano hinge to the edge of the door and the other leg to the inside edge of the cube. The plywood scraps and shims prop up the door at the correct height while the hinges are installed.

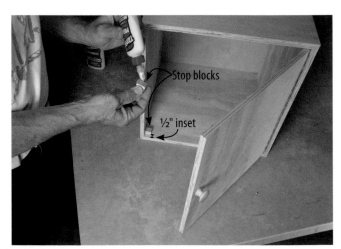

6 **ADD** a knob of your choice. Be creative (we weren't) since you can easily swap it out later for another knob. Glue on the little ¾" x ¾" stop blocks as shown.

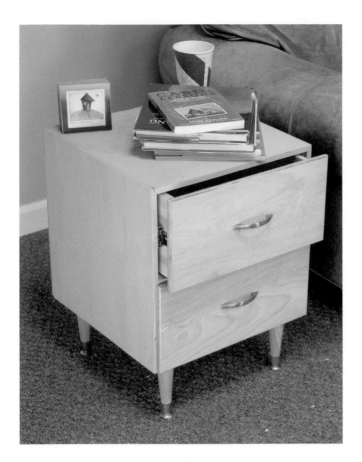

Build the Drawer Units

Cut the ¼" x ½" center dado as shown in Photo 7, then assemble the cube with the center divider in place. (The center divider will be the same dimensions as the top and bottom panels (B).

Next, build the drawers. The finished drawers must be 1" to 1⅛" narrower than the width of the opening so check this measurement and tweak your drawer dimensions as needed. Build the drawer boxes, then add the bottom as shown in Photo 8. We created rabbeted corners for strength but, again, you can alter the dimensions for parts J and K and use simpler butt joints.

Draw lines to indicate the centers of the drawer sides and the drawer opening. Install the drawer glides as shown in Photo 9. See "The Fine Art of Installing Drawer Glides" (p. 37) for more information. Test fit the drawers and adjust the glides as necessary so they operate smoothly.

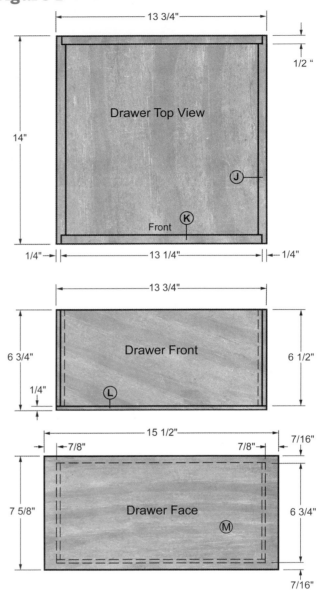

Figure 1

Cutting List for Drawers

Part	Dimensions	Qty
(J) Drawer side	½" x 6½" x 14"	2
(K) Drawer front/back	½" x 6½" x 13¼"	2
(L) Drawer bottom	¼" x 13⅝" x 14"	1
(M) Drawer face	½" x 7⅝" x 15½"	1

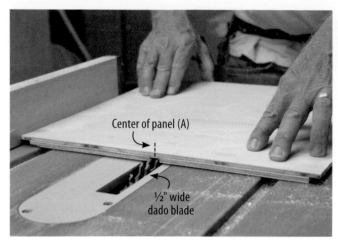

7 **CUT** ½" wide dadoes down the exact centers of the side pieces (A). Take your time setting the fence correctly so the drawer openings will be identical in size.

8 **BUILD** the drawers and install the ¼" bottoms to "square them up." Like the boxes, the side pieces are rabbeted to create stronger corner joints.

9 **INSTALL** the drawer glides. The ball-bearing tracks should be centered in the drawer opening and the slides should be centered on the drawer side.

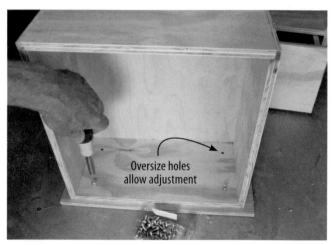

10 **SCREW** the fronts to the drawers using ¾" sheet metal screws driven through oversize holes; this extra "wiggle room" allows you to later adjust the drawer fronts if necessary.

Cut the drawer fronts to size and install them (Photo 10). Drill oversize holes and use ¾" long screws to install the fronts. The oversize holes allow you to adjust the fronts if they're slightly out of alignment. Add knobs and you're done.

Better-Looking Plywood Edges

The exposed edges of the plywood will most likely be porous and rough. Make an inexpensive "filler" by mixing a solution of ½ white glue, ½ water. "Paint" this solution on the exposed edges, then sand the edges with 120 grit sandpaper when the solution is dry. You may have to do this two or three times to fill extremely rough edges. This will help fill the pores and create a smoother edge for paint. Or you can simply apply several coats of paint, sanding in between, until the edges are smooth.

The Fine Art of Installing Drawer Glides

Building drawers used to strike terror into my heart; the tolerances seemed intolerable and the hardware looked complicated. But now that I've built a few hundred drawers I approach the task with Zen-like calm. Here are a few tips:

- Almost all glides are ½" thick meaning your drawer needs to be at least 1" narrower than the opening. I say "at least" because if you make the drawers too wide, you've got a problem. There's no easy way to adjust the drawer, glide or box to create a larger opening. I usually make my drawers about 1⅛" narrower than the opening then make minor adjustments as described next.

- Most glides—the part you secure to the box—have adjustable tongues that can be slightly bent to effectively narrow the opening. I drive the mounting screws in the "loose ends" of these tongues so the slide can be slightly moved in or out. You can also use cardboard or wood shims to narrow the opening.

- Mount both sides of the glide smack dab in the middle of the drawer and the opening; there's less chance of error than mounting them near the top or bottom.

- The "slide" part that mounts to the drawer side has both vertical and horizontal oblong holes. I use the vertical ones so I can use them to adjust the drawer slightly up or down as needed.

- When you slide the drawer into the opening for the first time, do it with a gentle touch. If you force it, you're likely to find a bunch of little ball bearings rolling all over the floor. If the drawer doesn't go in easily, the opening is most likely a little too large. If so, adjust the tongues on the glides to make the opening smaller. As discussed, if you've made the opening too narrow your only alternative is to rebuild the drawer box.

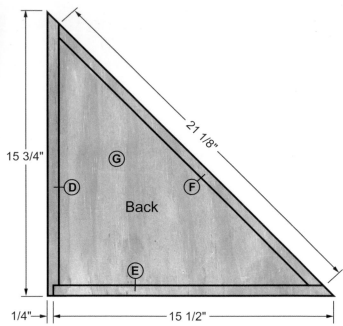

15 3/4"

21 1/8"

(G)

(D)   (F)

Back

(E)

1/4" → ←— 15 1/2" —→

Cutting List for Triangular Units

Part	Dimensions	Qty
(D) Side #1	½" x 15¾" x 15½" *	1
(E) Side #2	½" x 15½" x 15½" **	1
(F) Hypotenuse	½" x 21⅛" x 15½" ***	1
(G) Back	¼" x 15¾" x 15¾"	1

*Square end to 45-degree end; square end is rabbeted
**Square end to 45-degree end
***45-degree end to 45-degree end

Build the Triangular Units

The triangular units are exactly ½ the size of the cubes.

Start by cutting one of the backs (C) in half diagonally (Photo 11); this gives you a "base" for building the rest of the triangle. Cut the three sides of the triangle (D,E,F) to the dimensions given. Use a table saw set at 45 degrees (Photo 12) for accuracy. Finally, assemble the triangle as shown in Photo 13.

11 **CUT** a back panel (G) in half diagonally to create a base for building the triangular units.

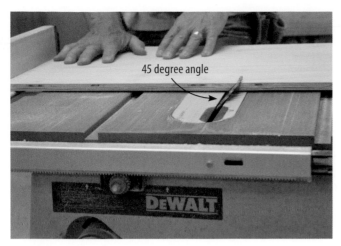

12 **CUT** 45 degree angles on the end (or ends) of three sides of the triangle. One end of part D also has a rabbet.

13 **ASSEMBLE** the triangle units using glue and nails.

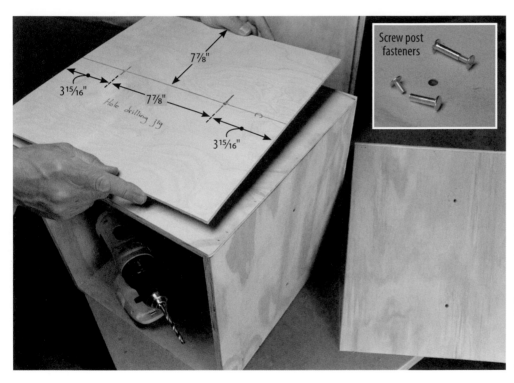

14 **CREATE** a hole-drilling template by boring two holes in a 15¾" x 15¾" square of plywood at the spacing shown. Use this template to bore holes in all four sides of each cube. The centerline of the template should be parallel with the front and back of the cube. The ¾" aluminum screw posts, when tightened, hold the two ½" sides tightly together.

Drill Holes for the Connectors

This is optional. The holes and connectors provide a way to temporarily—yet solidly—secure the cubes to one another as you reconfigure in different shapes. The connectors (inset) when installed through the holes of two adjoining cubes, will pull them tightly together.

Note: The holes won't align if the cubes are stacked in non-linear or rotated position.

If you don't want a bunch of holes in your cubes secure them to one another using ¾" screws. For truly permanent configurations, use construction adhesive.

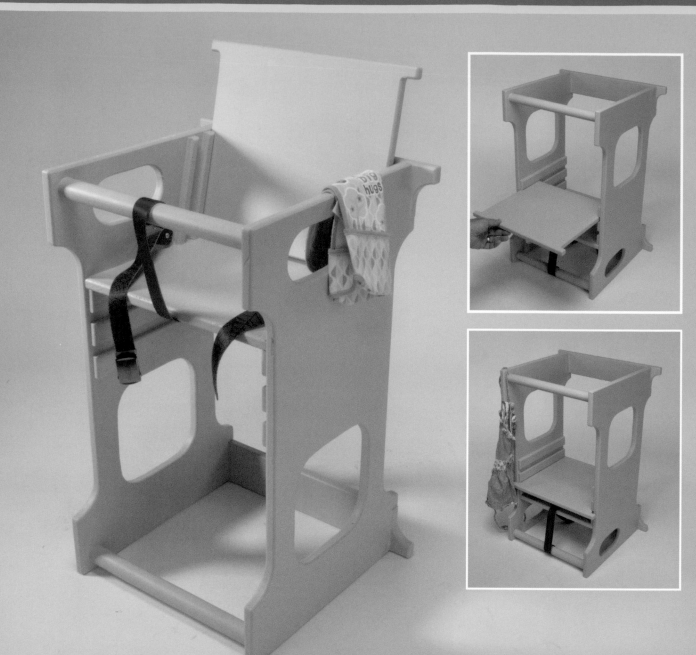

High Chair & Helper Stool

Upright for eating, upside down for helping

I was hanging out in one of my kids' already-too-small kitchens when I noticed they had both a high chair AND a helper tower crammed into one corner. I began thinking, wouldn't it be cool to have a single piece of furniture that could combine both functions? So I came up with this two-in-one kitchen helper. In the "upright" position it's a high chair that can be pulled up to the table. In the "upside down" position, it's a stool kids can stand on, without fear of toppling over backwards, while helping out. There's a movable panel (H) that can be slid into one set of slots

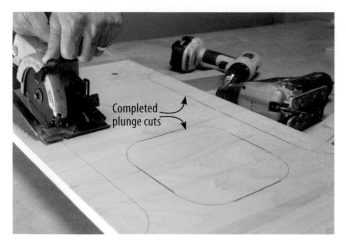

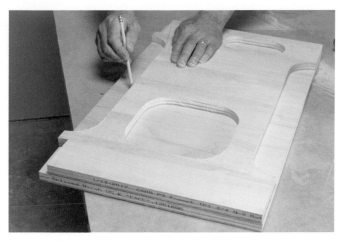

1 **CUT** out side panel A, after laying it out based on Figure 1. To make the plunge cut, position the blade over the cut line, retract the blade guard, then slowly but firmly lower the blade into the wood. Be careful—the saw can kick back. If you're not comfortable doing this, make your cuts with a jigsaw.

2 **USE** side panel A as a pattern for side panel B. Round over the edges of the plywood with a router and ¼" round over bit.

to create a higher back for the high chair, and slid into another set of slots to raise the platform in "kitchen helper" mode.

We're providing dimensions for a tower that will work with most 30" high tables and 36" counters—but not all tables, counters or kids for that matter, are created equal. Do your own measuring and head scratching; you may want to adjust some dimensions to better suit your situation.

How to Build It

Follow the measurements in Figure 1 to layout side panel A. Use a circular saw to make the straight cuts and a jigsaw to cut the curves (Photo 1). Sand any rough or uneven edges. Trace this shape onto the second plywood panel (B) as shown in Photo 2. Rout the edges of both sides of both panels.

Use 2" screws to secure the seat (C) in place (Photo 3). A couple of clamps come in handy here. Use a square to ensure the parts are square to one another as you work. Flip the

Figure 1

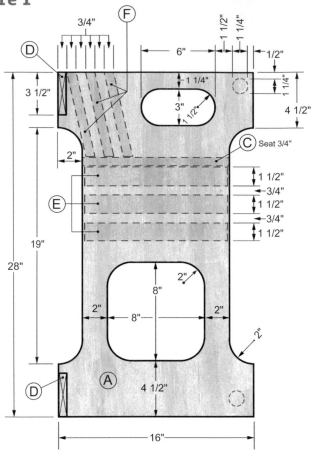

Figure 2

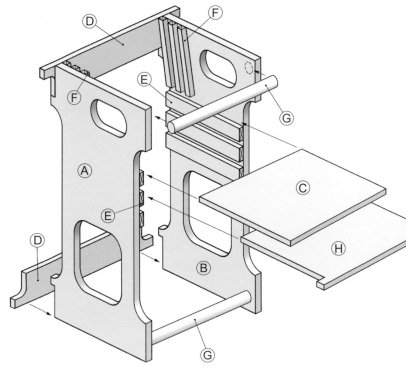

Cutting List

Part	Dimensions	Qty
(A) Left side panel	¾" x 16" x 28"	1
(B) Right side panel	¾" x 16" x 28"	1
(C) Seat	¾" x 12" x 14"	1
(D) Top, bottom wings	¾" x 3½" x 18½"	2
(E) Platform supports	½" x 1½" x 11½"	6
(F) Angled back supports	½" x ¾" x 7" *	4
(G) Cross dowels	1¼" x 14"	2
(H) Moveable panel	¾" x 15½" x 13⅞"	1

* Ends cuts are 12 degrees

Materials List

Material	Qty
¾" x 4' x 4' AC or better plywood	1
1 x 4 x 4' pine	1
½" x 1½" x 6' pine	1
½" x ¾" x 3' pine	1
1¼" x 36" dowel (or closet pole rod)	1
Fasteners: 2" all-purpose screws, 1" brad nails, wood glue	

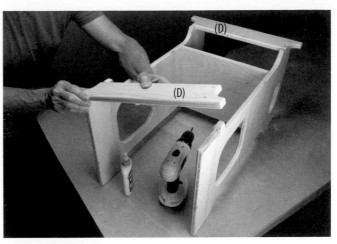

3 **SCREW** the seat (C) to the side panels. Use clamps to hold the parts together and a square to keep the parts square to one another as you work.

4 **INSTALL** the top and bottom wings in the notches cut at the tops and bottoms of the side panels. Secure with glue and screws.

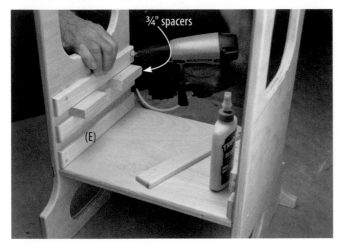

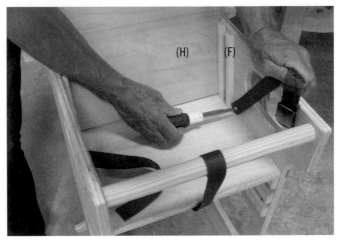

5 **NAIL** the platform supports (E) to the side panels. Use ¾" thick scraps as spacers to ensure the supports are the correct distance apart. Add the angled back supports (F) using the same procedure.

6 **SECURE** the cross dowels at the top and bottom of the chair. Attach the safety belt sections to the chair using flat head screws.

tower onto its tummy and secure the top and bottom wings (D) into the notches (Photo 4).

Use glue and finish nails to install the platform supports (E) as shown in Photo 5. There are three pairs of supports so the platform can be raised to three different heights as needed. Use the same procedure to install the multiple angled back supports (F).

Install the cross dowels (G) adding a finish nail in one end to prevent spinning. Finally install the "kid tie down" straps (Photo 6). We

got all three parts from a single belt; find or buy one with a buckle that's easy for you to fasten, but difficult for your kid to unfasten. We cut 12" off both the buckle and insert ends, then used the remaining center section for the strap that runs from the center of the cross dowel to the center of the seat. Secure all the ends with ⅝" screws with large heads. Apply your finish of choice. Chow time.

Jumping Jack Table & Stools

Fun to use, cheap to build, easy to store

Kids love to entertain real friends, make-believe friends, dolls and themselves. This table set is ideal for all those occasions. Plus, the table and stools are easy to "unslot" for storing.

How to Build the Table

Layout the plywood as shown in Figure 1. We traced around a 4-in. diameter roll of duct tape to create the curves for the feet, "armpits," "hands" and "crotch" of Jumping Jack. The two leg sections are identical with the exception of the location of the connecting slots. Use a circular saw (Photo 1) and jigsaw to cut out the parts; fine-tooth blades in both will give you the cleanest cuts.

Sand the edges as shown in Photo 2. Use whatever sanders—hand or power—you have to get the job done.

Use a router with a ¼" round over bit to soften all the edges (Photo 3), *except* for the notches, feet bottoms and flat top where the tabletop will rest. Sand and rout all four edges of the tabletop.

Slide the slots into one another as shown in Photo 4. If the tops don't align, slightly deepen one or both slots. Secure the triangular mounting blocks (C), cut from scrap, to the underside of the table (Photo 5), then position the legs and secure them with a few screws. Add the optional leg blocking (D) as shown in Photo 6. The blocks help minimize leg wobble and create mini-shelves for stashing stuff—but they also make it more difficult to disassemble the table for storage—so you choose.

How to Build the Stools

The construction of the stools mimics the steps used for the table. Layout the stools (Photo 7) as shown in Figure 2. You'll be able to get three from the plywood left over from the table. If you want a fourth stool, you'll need to buy an extra 2' x 4' piece of plywood.

Follow all the other steps you did for the table. Secure the seat to the mounting blocks, then check the stools for rocking. If you have wobble, put shims or coins under the short legs, then mark the longer legs (Photo 8) and trim them to length.

Parts List ("Qty" per table or stool)

Part	Dimensions	Qty
(A) Table legs	¾" x 20" x 35"	2
(B) Tabletop	¾" x 24½" x 24½"	1
(C) Tabletop blocking	¾" x 6" x 8" triangle	2
(D) Table Leg Blocking (opt.)	¾" x 6" x 8" triangle	4
(E) Stool legs	¾" x 14" x 16½"	2
(F) Stool seat	¾" x 14" x 14"	1
(G) Stool blocking	¾" x 6" x 8" triangle	2

Materials List (provides for 1 table and 3 stools)

Material	Qty
¾" x 4' x 8' maple, birch Appleply or other plywood	1

Figure 1: Table

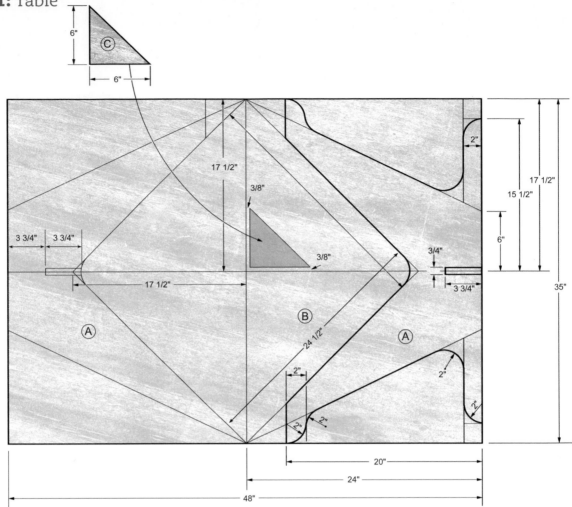

Figure 2: Stool

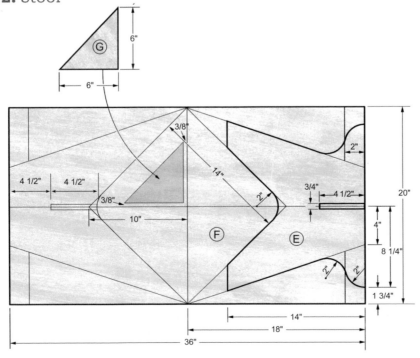

1 CUT OUT the plywood based on the measurements in the diagram. Use a fine-tooth circular saw for straight cuts and fine-tooth jigsaw blade for curves.

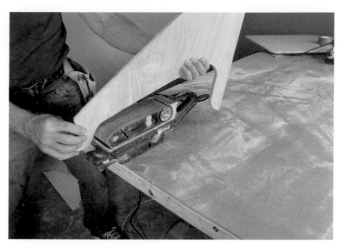

2 SAND the edges smooth with a power sander, drill-powered sanding drum or sandpaper wrapped around a block.

3 ROUND OVER all of the edges—except for the tops of the arms, the slots and the bottoms of the feet—using a router and ¼" round over bit.

4 SLIDE the slots together. If the tops of the arms don't lie flat against the table, deepen one or both notches slightly.

5 PLOP the leg assembly onto the underside of the top, nestled between two triangular mounting blocks (C). Secure the legs to the blocks with a few screws.

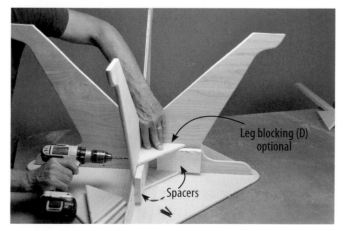

6 ADD the optional leg blocking to minimize wobble and provide mini shelves. Use 1x4 spacers to position the blocking; adjacent blocks will be offset ¾" making it easier to screw them to the legs.

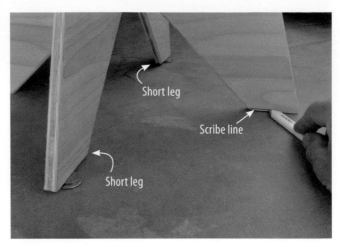

7 **LAYOUT** three stools on the remaining section of plywood, following the same procedures you did for the table.

8 **SCRIBE** the legs to remove any "rocking action." Shim up the two short legs, evenly (we used coins), then mark and cut the two longer legs.

Short leg

Scribe line

Short leg

Dress Up Your Table and Chairs

This dining room set got its name because the table legs look like they're doing jumping jack exercises. We were tempted to paint socks and tennis shoes on the feet and gym shorts on the legs! You don't have to paint exercise clothes on your table and stools, but you can sure have a lot of fun painting each stool and/or each component a different color!

QUICK TIP

If you have a flat top belt sander like ours, set it upside down on the workbench and use it as a bench sander.

LEGO & Game Table

A place to build and store—plus a flip top for other fun and games

It's estimated over 600 billion LEGO© parts have been made since the first one rolled off the assembly in Denmark in 1949. This table won't store all of them, but it'll store a few hundred. Plus it will provide a sturdy platform for building mega structures. As a bonus, you can flip over the top and have a game table for playing checkers and other games.

Top View

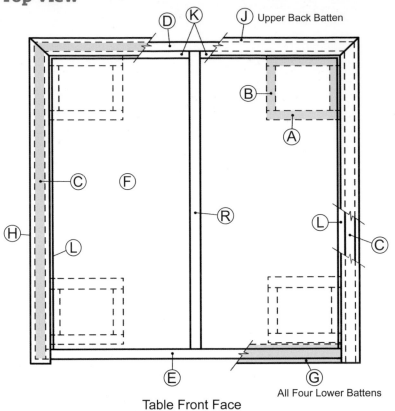

Upper Back Batten

Table Front Face

All Four Lower Battens

Cutting List

Part	Dimensions	Qty
(A) Leg	¾" x 5½" x 12"	8
(B) Leg	¾" x 3½" x 12"	8
(C) Box side	¾" x 3½" x 24"	2
(D) Box back	¾" x 3½" x 22½"	1
(E) Box front	¾" x 2⅝" x 22½"	1
(F) Bottom	⅜" x 22½" x 22½" (plywood)	1
(G) Lower battens	⅜" x 1½" x 24¾"*	4
(H) Upper side battens	⅜" x 1½" x 24⅜"	2
(J) Upper back batten	⅜" x 1½" x 24¾" *	1
(K) Back runner	⅜" x ⅜" x 22½"	1
(L) Side runners	⅜" x ⅜" x 22"	2
(M) Sliding lid base	⅜" x 22⅜" x 25"	1
(N) Lid back trim	⅜" x 1" x 22⅜"	1
(O) Lid side trim	⅜" x 1" x 20"	2
(P) Lid front trim	⅜" x 3¾" x 22⅜"	1
(Q) LEGO© panels	10" x 10"	4
(R) Partition	¾" x 2⅝" x 22½"	1

Long point to long point

Sliding Top: Cross Section

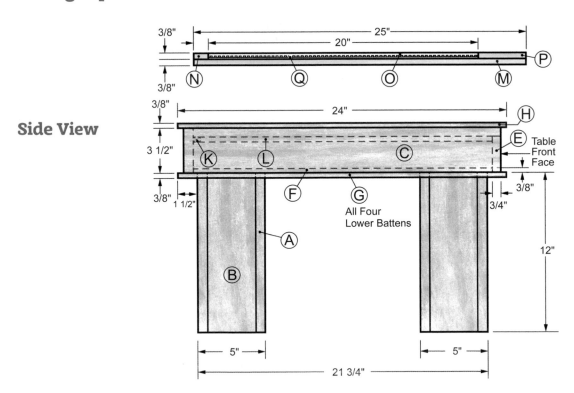

Side View

All Four Lower Battens

Table Front Face

1 CUT eight 1x6s (A) and eight 1x4s (B) to length using a miter saw or a circular saw guided by a Speed Square.

2 BUILD the legs with the 1x4s sandwiched between the 1x6s; they won't be perfectly square, but they'll be close. Use glue and 6d finish nails to secure the parts to one another.

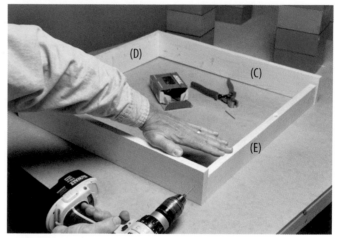

3 PAINT the legs. Make lines at 3" increments to act as guides. We "rough sprayed" the top and middle area, then masked them off and sprayed the remaining sections as shown.

4 CONSTRUCT the storage box. Cut ⅞" off the front piece to allow room for the top to slide in and out.

How to Build It

Cut the leg components (A, B) to length as shown in Photo 1; a miter saw is faster, but a circular saw guided by a square will work too. Assemble the four legs (Photo 2) using glue and 4d finish nails. Predrill the holes if necessary to prevent splitting.

Spray paint the legs to look like a LEGO blocks (Photo 3). Select whatever colors you want (or have) and use masking tape to create crisp edges. Once the paint is dry, draw lines with a marking pen to separate the colored "blocks."

Build the storage box (C, D, E) as shown in Photo 4. The front board (E) is shallower to provide an exit space for the top.

QUICK TIP

If you lack the correct drill bit, nip the head off a finish nail and use that.

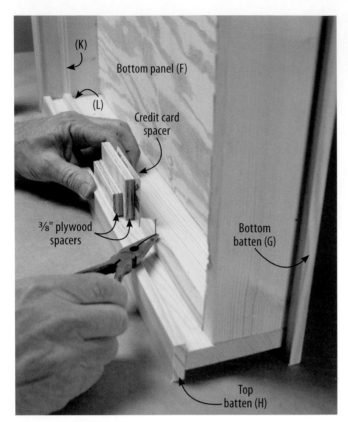

Labels in image: (K), Bottom panel (F), (L), Credit card spacer, ⅜" plywood spacers, Bottom batten (G), Top batten (H)

5 **INSTALL** the battens and runners. Nail the battens along three edges of the top and all four edges of the bottom. Make sure to install the bottom panel (F) before you install the runners.

Nail the four bottom battens (G) and three top battens (H, J) to the box, then glue and nail the bottom panel (F) to the bottom battens. Secure the narrow runners (K, L) to the sides as shown in Photo 5. Use two scraps of ⅜" plywood plus a credit card as spacers to create a slot wide enough for the ¾" thick top to slide freely. Add the center partition (R) to divide up the space and create an extra support for the sliding top.

Build the top as shown (M, N, O, P) as shown in Photo 6. Use construction adhesive to secure the plastic base panels and wood glue and small brads to secure the plywood surround pieces. Finally, install the legs (Photo 7) using wood glue and drywall screws. Then break out the LEGOs or game boards and start playing!

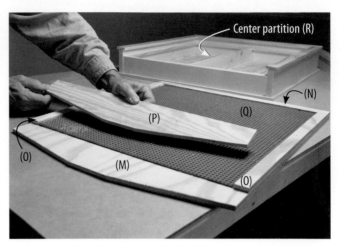

Labels in image: Center partition (R), (N), (P), (Q), (O), (M), (O)

6 **BUILD** the top. Secure the four base panels to the plywood top using construction adhesive, surround them on three sides with strips of plywood, then install the tongue (P).

7 **SCREW** the legs to the box. The outside corners of the legs should fit snuggly against the inside corners of the battens.

Workbench Trivia

The LEGO group was founded in 1932 in the workshop of Ole Christiansen, a carpenter and wooden toy maker. In 1949, they began manufacturing the first "Automatic Binding Blocks." Seventy years later, a life-size version of an X-wing fighter, containing over 5 million LEGO blocks—the largest LEGO block model ever created—was displayed in New York City.

Little Lounger

A pint-size chair, a pint-size project

Here's a project that's little in every way. It's for little people, only takes a little lumber and time to build—and if you have little experience—this is a great little project. The chair components are cut from three boards and you only need a handful of tools to build it.

Cutting List

Part	Dimension	Qty
(A) Long leg	2" x 4" x 42" (long to short of 45º)	2
(B) Short leg	2" x 6" x 16¾" (long to short of 45º)	2
(C) Rear seat slat	2" x 6" x 16"	1
(D) Front seat slat	2" x 6" x 19"	1
(E) Back slats	5⁄4" x 2⅝" x 19"	7
(F) Back slat (top)	5⁄4" x 5½" x 19"	1
(G) Footrest	5⁄4" x 2⅝" x 19"	1

Materials List

Material	Qty
2 x 6 x 8' cedar board	1
2 x 4 x 8' cedar board	1
5⁄4" x 6" x 8' cedar deck board	2
2½" exterior screws (1 lb.), water resistant glue	

We used cedar because of its superior weather resistance, but you can use treated lumber (and spend about ⅓ less) or even pine if you plan to use it indoors. So, let's roll up those little sleeves and get building.

How to Build It

Cut the two 2x4 long legs (A) and two 2x6 short legs (B) to length. Position the boards (Photo 1) so the short angle of the back leg "kisses" the back edge of the front leg when the bottoms of the boards are aligned. (The "nose" of the 2x6 will protrude past the front of the 2x4.) Note the assemblies are mirror images of one another; you *don't* want to end up with two left or two right sides! Secure the parts using waterproof glue and exterior screws.

Use clamps to hold your leg assemblies upright (Photo 2), then install the two seat boards (C, D). The back board (C) fits between the front legs, the front board (D) sits even with the outside edges of the front legs. Rout the edges of the front board before assembly.

The back slats (E) are made by ripping 5 ½" wide deck boards in half. Cut the boards to length, rip them down the middle using a table saw or circular saw with a straight cutting guide (see page 104), then soften the edges using a ½" round over router bit. Install the slats using carpenters' pencils (about ¼") as spacers. Predrill holes to avoid splitting. Before screwing the slats down, lay them all out on the 2x4 back supports and tweak the spacing so the arched top slat (F) winds up in the position shown in diagram.

Install the footrest (G) as shown in Photo 4. Predrill holes (like I *should* have) to avoid splitting the ends.

Apply a clear exterior finish if you want to hang on to that rich cedar color.

Figure 1: Side View

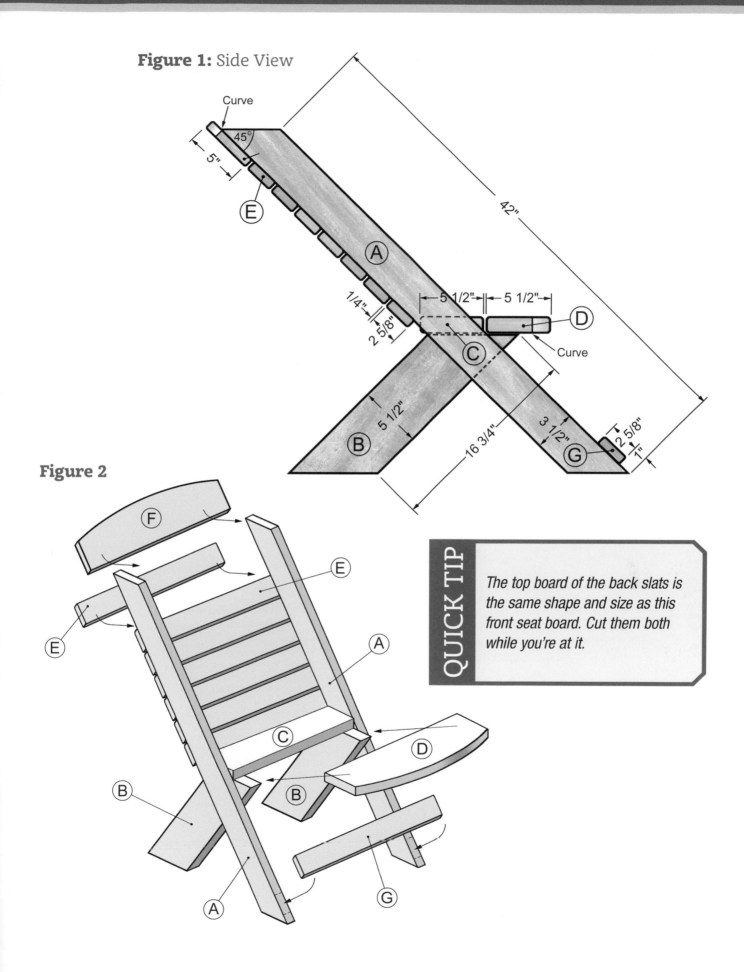

Curve

45°

5"

E

42"

A

1/4"

2 5/8"

5 1/2" | 5 1/2"

D

Curve

C

5 1/2"

B

16 3/4"

3 1/2"

G

2 5/8"

1"

Figure 2

F

E

E

A

E

C

D

B

B

G

A

QUICK TIP

The top board of the back slats is the same shape and size as this front seat board. Cut them both while you're at it.

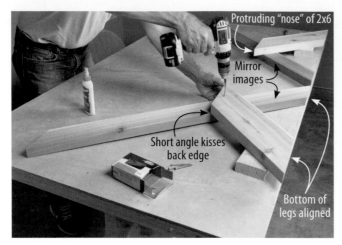

1 SCREW the back legs to the front legs, applying waterproof glue beforehand for added strength. Make sure the assemblies are mirror images of one another.

2 INSTALL the two seat boards. Usa a jigsaw to cut the curved front piece and a router with a roundover bit to soften the edges.

3 SECURE the back slats to the backside of the 2x4 supports. Use a carpenter's pencil (about ¼") as a spacer to ensure consistent spacing.

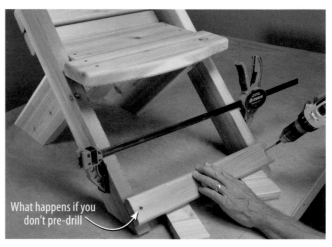

4 SCREW the front brace in place. Apply a clear finish or leave the cedar unfinished so it fades into a mellow gray.

Just the Right Size

Just for fun I built an adult-size version of this little lounger—and it's surprisingly comfortable. We don't provide the dimensions for the large-scale version, but have at it if you're inclined.

Smart Tips for Kid-Safe Furniture

Building colorful, unique furniture is fun; building furniture that's functional is important, but building kids' furniture that's *safe* is critical. And safety doesn't end when you leave the workshop; it's imperative furniture be installed and used correctly.

Here are some safety tips related to kids' furniture—whether you buy it or build it. There's more detailed information on the Consumer Product Safety Commission website at www.cpsc.gov.

Always secure dressers, bookcases, cabinets and desks to walls. Failure to do this is the number one cause of furniture-related accidents. Kids can pull out drawers and use them as steps for reaching items higher up. Or use shelves as ladders for climbing. Secure furniture to wall studs with at least two safety brackets or straps; they're reasonably priced, easy to install and available everywhere. (**Photo A**)

Position your TVs safely. The popularity of flat-screen TVs has created two problems. First, thin TVs can be set on narrow furniture which is more tippy. Second, when people purchase flat-screen TVs, they often relegate their old "big box" TVs to other parts of the house—and those new locations often have furniture that wasn't designed to accommodate big, heavy items.

Install safety latches and hinges on chests to prevent lids from falling freely and slamming fingers or other body parts. And never install locking mechanisms. (**Photo B**)

Create finger cut outs in chest fronts. Cutouts minimize the chance of fingers getting pinched, eliminate the need for knobs and provide plenty of ventilation if someone gets inside.

Round corners and round over sharp edges. Crisp edges and corners may look nice, but they can cut or bruise when banged into. Use a jigsaw and router with a round over bit to soften these areas. (**Photo C**)

Prevent head entrapment. Consumer Product Safety Commission guidelines state the space between cradle spindles shouldn't exceed 2⅜" (if I soda can will fit between the spindles the spaces are too big). They also specify no cutouts in the headboards or footboards. (**Photo D**)

Use non-toxic finishes. Most finishes today are non-toxic when allowed to cure and harden properly—but read labels to make sure. One super safe finish on natural wood is salad bowl oil.

Be alert in other people's homes; they may not be as scrupulous in child-proofing their home and furniture as you.

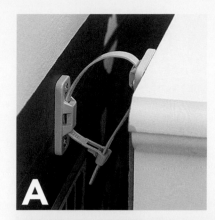

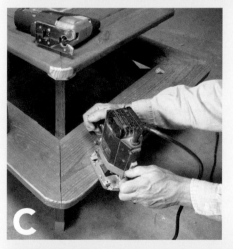

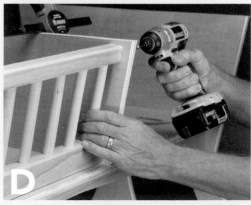

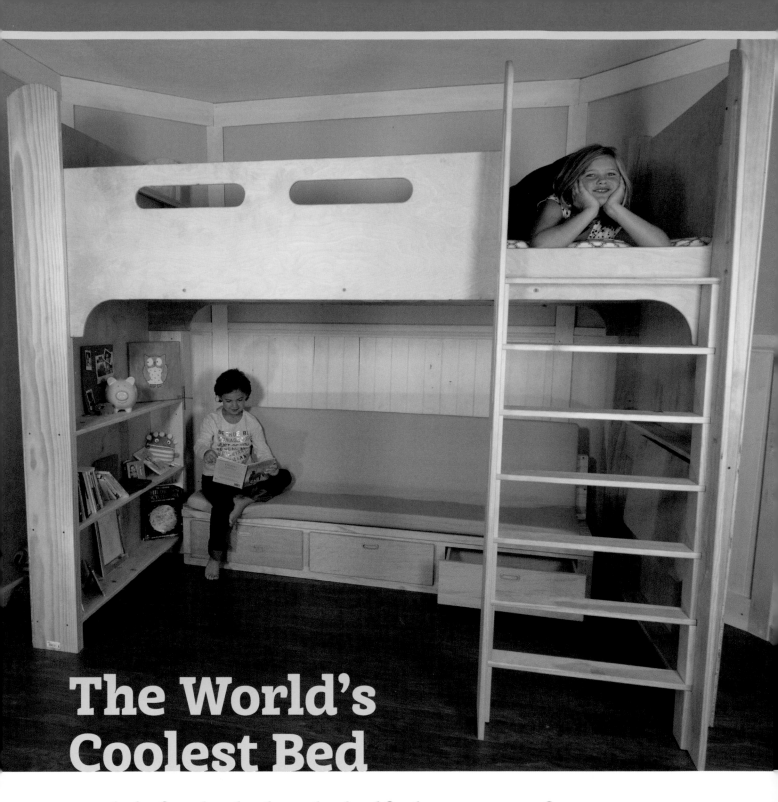

The World's Coolest Bed

Bed, loft, desk, bookshelf, dresser, sofa, guest bedroom—and a secret chamber—rolled into one

Parents love loft beds because they solve a problem: They get the bed up and out of the way to provide more floor space for dressers, bookshelves and other kid stuff (especially useful in small bedrooms.) Kids love them for a quite different reason: They're just flat out fun.

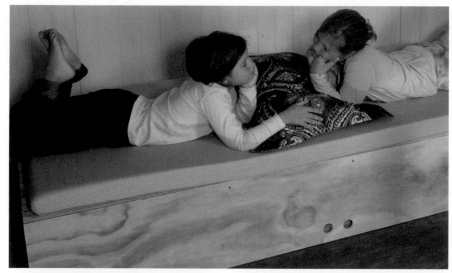

This loft bed packs a whallop. It features:

- **A raised bed** that's easy to get in and out of, yet has sturdy side rails to prevent "rollovers."
- **A sofa** that flips into a guest bed.
- **Built-in shelves** for stashing books, toys and stuffed animals
- **A flip-up desk** for doing homework or art projects
- **A cabinet headboard** with sliding doors (and a secret compartment.)

One of the beauties of this project is you can build as much or as little of it as you want. Or add the other elements over time.

Build the Basic Bed Framework

This is the meat and potatoes of the project. Height-wise, it's designed to fit a space with 8-ft. ceilings—if you have taller ceilings you can modify some dimensions to create more headroom above and below.

Start by building the four legs—two are 7¼" wide, the others 3½". Cut the four legs (A,B) to length then, starting at the bottom, glue and nail the blocking to them (Photo 1). Use a spacer block to create the ¾" space that will accommodate the ends of the shelves. Screw the shelves in place as shown in Photo 2. If all of your measurements are correct, the leg assemblies will wind up a convenient 48" in width.

Figure 1: Loft Bed

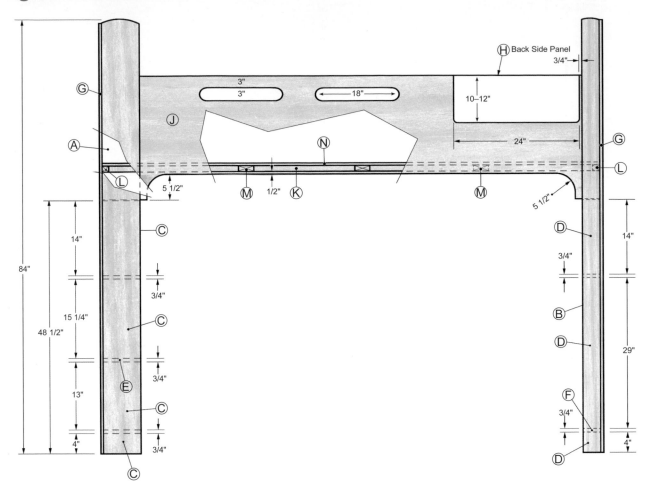

Parts & Cutting List (Bed Loft Unit)

Part	Dimension	Qty
(A) Wide leg	1⅛" x 7¼" x 84"*	2
(B) Narrow leg	1⅛" x 3½" x 84"*	2
(C) Wide leg blocking	¾" x 7¼" x varies	6
(D) Narrow leg blocking	¾" x 3½" x varies	varies
(E) Wide leg shelves	¾" x 7¼" x 45¾"	varies
(F) Narrow leg shelves	¾" x 3½" x 45¾"	varies
(G) Leg panels	½" x 48" x 82"	2
(H) Back side panel	¾" x 24" x 96"	1
(J) Front side panel	¾" x 24" x 96"	1
(K) Long mattress support	¾" x 1½" x 96"	2
(L) Short mattress support	¾" x 1½" x 42¾"	2
(M) Intermediate mattress support	1½" x 3½" x 42¾"	3
(N) Plywood mattress support	½" x 44¼" x 96"	1

Bed mattress: We used a LUCID 5-inch Gel Memory Foam Mattress, Dual layered, Twin XL size from Amazon.com (around $110)

*May need to be special ordered

Cut the leg panels (G) to length and cut the little leg cutouts in the bottom. Secure the panels to the leg assemblies using glue and trim head screws. The panels will automatically square up the leg assembly.

Cut the side panels (H, J) as shown in Figure 1 and Photos 4 & 5. Enlist a helper to help you stand the two leg panels about 8 feet apart, rest the side panels on the uppermost blocking, then screw the panels to the legs as shown in Photo 6. Make sure the ends of the side panels sit square to the end leg assemblies and use plenty of screws. The more secure these side panels, the more rock solid and wiggle-free the loft will be.

Build the large rectangular mattress framework (K, L, M) on the ground then

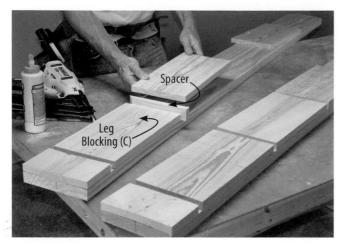

1 **SECURE** the leg blocking (C) to the leg using glue and finish nails. Use a ¾" spacer block to ensure the shelves will fit snugly.

2 **SCREW** the shelves to the legs using 3-in all-purpose screws. The shelves provide storage and extra strength to the leg assemblies.

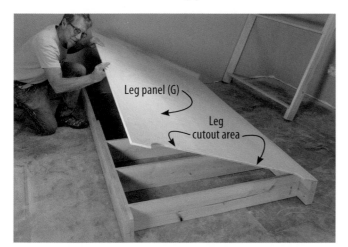

3 **CUT** the leg panels to the correct length and shape, then test fit them before installing them permanently with wood glue and trim head screws.

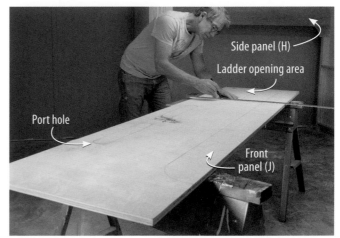

4 **LAYOUT** the horizontal front and back panels (H, J). The back panel has only an arched bottom; the front also has cutouts for the ladder and "port holes."

(hopefully that helper is still around) lift the framework into place, clamp it at the right elevation, then secure it with screws. Once the frame is in place drive ¼" x 3" lag screws through the plywood sides and into the ends of all three mattress supports (M). Someday you're going to find 6 kids sitting in the loft and you'll be glad you added these screws. Drop the plywood bottom (N) in place and your main structure is complete.

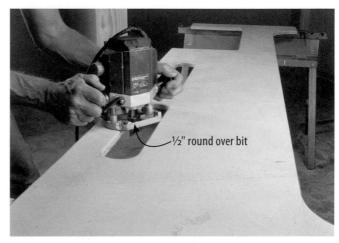

5 **ROUND** OVER all the edges using a router and round over bit.

Side panels rest on blocking

6 **SCREW** the front panel to the legs. Note the ends of both panels are supported by the uppermost blocks. These panels stabilize the bed, support the mattress framework and provide safety rails—all in one fell swoop.

(L)

(K) (M)

Mattress support frame

7 **BUILD** the plywood and mattress support frame on the ground, then lift it into place in one piece and install screws. Once it's in place drive ¼" x 3" lag screws through the plywood sides into the ends of the 2x4 mattress supports (M).

Build the Ladder

Purchase clear, knot-free lumber for the ladder parts. You'll pay more, but you—and whoever is sleeping in the loft—will sleep better knowing there's a solidly-built ladder in place. Cut the rails (0) to the length, angle and shape shown in Figure 2. Make the cutouts for the handrail using a 1¼" drill bit to create the rounded ends of the three openings (Photo 8).

Figure 2:
Ladder

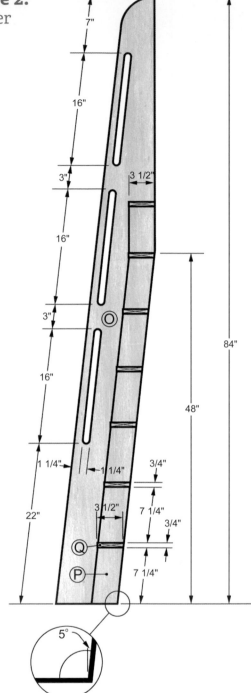

7"
16"
3"
3 1/2"
16"
3"
16"
84"
48"
1 1/4"
1 1/4"
3/4"
22"
3 1/2"
7 1/4"
3/4"
Q
7 1/4"
P
5°

Parts & Cutting List (Ladder)

Part	Dimension	Qty
(0) Ladder rails	¾" x 7¼" x 84" (5° bottom cut)	2
(P) Rung blocking	¾" x 3½" x 7¼' (5° end cuts)	7
(Q) Rungs	¾" x 3½" x 24"	7

"End holes" for railing

QUICK TIP

We built our ladder at a relatively steep 5° angle to conserve floor space. If space isn't an issue you can use the same basic technique to construct a less-steep 10° or 15° ladder.

8 **LAYOUT** and cut the ladder rails (0) as shown in Figure 2. The integral handrails are created by cutting oblong openings in the upper edge of the rails.

Rung blocking (P)

Rungs (Q)

9 **BUILD** the ladder by alternately installing rung blocking (P) and rungs (Q). Secure the blocking to the rails with glue and finish nails. Secure the rungs with finish nails driven into the tops of the blocking they rest on.

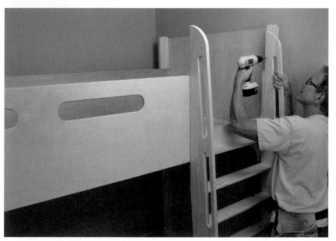

10 **INSTALL** the ladder. Secure the right side to the bed leg and the left side to the front panel using all-purpose screws.

Position the rails across from one another (Photo 9) then—starting at the bottom—alternately install the rung blocking (P) and the rungs (Q). Use glue and nails to secure the blocks to the rails, then secure the rungs to the blocks they're resting on using 6d finish nails.

Build the Flip Desk

This flip-up desk is optional and you can build it almost any size, shape and height you want…thus no materials or parts lists. The "almost" comes into play in regards to swing clearance; make sure the desktop can swing up without hitting the sofa bed. Buy your folding shelf brackets and experiment with the desktop width and mounting height before permanently installing the brackets.

We installed a horizontal 1x6 just below the mid-level shelf on the "ladder side" of the bed and secured our brackets as shown in Photo 12. Adjust the height based on who's using it and what they'll be sitting on.

Build the Sofa-Bed-Drawer Unit

This part of the project is the most challenging, but when you're done you'll have a piece of furniture that functions as a sofa, a flip down guest bed and a chest of drawers.

Begin by making the drawer unit face frame (Figure 3). Cut your stiles (BB) to length and drill pairs of "pocket holes" as shown in photo 13. (*Note:* For more detailed information on using pocket screws visit YouTube). Cut the rails (AA) to length then secure the stiles to them with glue and pocket screws (Photo 14).

Build the four dividers and end panels as shown in Photo 15 and install them as shown in Photo 16. Install the bench back (FF) and top (GG) to complete the bench part of the project.

Your next mission is to build the flip-down combination seat-backrest. If you cut and assemble everything correctly, the seat-backrest in the "flipped down" position will create a flat bed and when "flipped up" will provide the bench backrest; keep this in mind as you

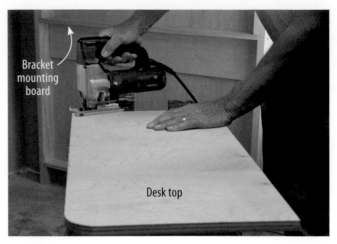

11 **CUT** the desktop to the desired size and shape. The primary consideration is that it won't interfere with the sofa-drawer unit when each are flipped up or down.

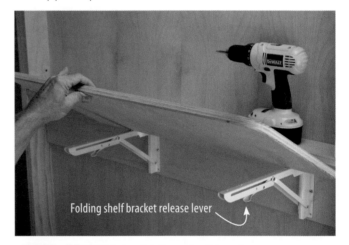

12 **SECURE** the folding shelf brackets to a horizontal 1x6, then secure the top to the brackets.

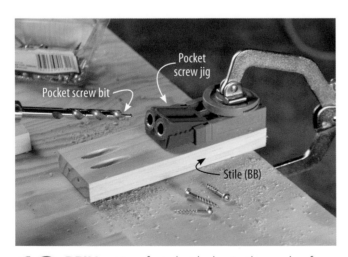

13 **DRILL** pairs of pocket holes in the ends of the short bench stiles (BB) using the special pocket hole jig, bit and clamp.

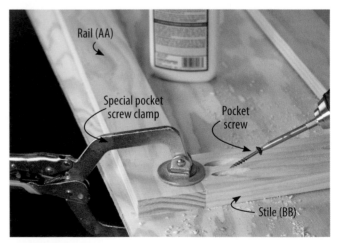

14 **DRIVE** pocket screws through stiles (BB) into the long rails (AA). Apply glue to the ends of the stiles beforehand to create a solid connection.

Figure 3: Sofa Bed

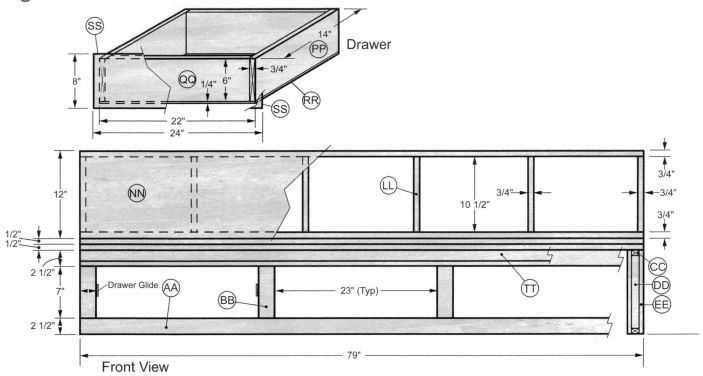

Drawer

Front View

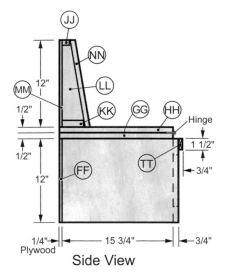

Side View

check and double check measurements as you build—especially if you're modifying the size.

Cut the seat top plate (JJ), seat bottom plate (KK) and backrest ribs (LL) to length. Taper cut the backrest ribs and secure them to the rails as seen in Photo 17. Use wood glue and drywall screws to secure the seat base (HH), backrest back (MM) and backrest front (NN). Position the seat assembly (Photo 18) and connect it to the bench assembly with the piano hinges (OO).

Parts & Cutting List (Sofa)

Part	Dimension	Qty
(AA) Bench rails	¾" x 2½" x 79"	2
(BB) Bench stiles	¾" x 2½" x 7"	4
(CC) Divider bottom/top plate	¾" x 1½" x 15¾"	8
(DD) Divider upright	¾" x 1½" x 10½"	8
(EE) Divider side panels	½" x 12" x 15¾"	8
(FF) Bench back	¼" x 12" x 79"	1
(GG) Bench top	½" x 16¾" x 79"	1
(HH) Seat base	½" x 16¾" x 79"	1
(JJ) Seat top plate	¾" x 1½" x 79"	1
(KK) Seat bottom plate	¾" x 3½" x 79"	1
(LL) Backrest ribs	¾" x 3½" x 10½" (tapered)*	6
(MM) Backrest back	¼" x 12" x 79"	1
(NN) Backrest front	½" x 12¼" x 79"	1
(OO) Piano hinge	48" and 30"	1/ea.
(PP) Drawer side	½" x 6" x 14"	6
(QQ) Drawer front/back	½" x 6" x 21"	6
(RR) Drawer bottom	¼" x 14" x 22"	3
(SS) Drawer face	½' x 8" x 24"	3
(TT) Front trim	¾" x 1½" x 79"	1

Sofa mattress: Simmons Beauty Sleep Siesta 3" Memory Foam mattress, roll-up bed, Twin size sold by Marketing Allegiance (through Amazon) (around $75)
*Tapers from 1½" to 3½"

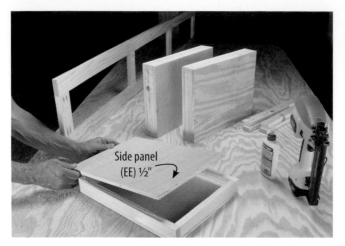

15 **BUILD** the dividers and end panels using glue and finish nails. Use the side panels (EE) to square up the dividers.

Side panel (EE) ½"

Stiles

Bench back (FF)

16 **SECURE** the dividers to the face frame. The edges of the dividers should align exactly with the edges of the stiles.

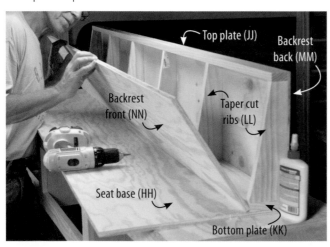

Top plate (JJ)

Backrest back (MM)

Backrest front (NN)

Taper cut ribs (LL)

Seat base (HH)

Bottom plate (KK)

17 **BUILD** the seat-backrest assembly. The taper cut ribs serve as backrest in the flipped-up position, legs in the flipped-down position.

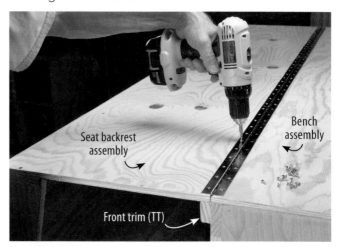

Seat backrest assembly

Bench assembly

Front trim (TT)

18 **SECURE** the seat-backrest assembly to the bench assembly using 48" and 30" piano hinges. Install front trim (TT) beforehand to help support the seat-backrest assembly during installation.

19 **ASSEMBLE** the three drawers. If you've taken care to create three identical drawer openings, you can create three identical drawers.

20 **INSTALL** the drawer glides, drawers and drawer faces. Select and install drawer pulls that don't extend too far creating a "snagging hazard."

Figure 4: Sliding Door Unit

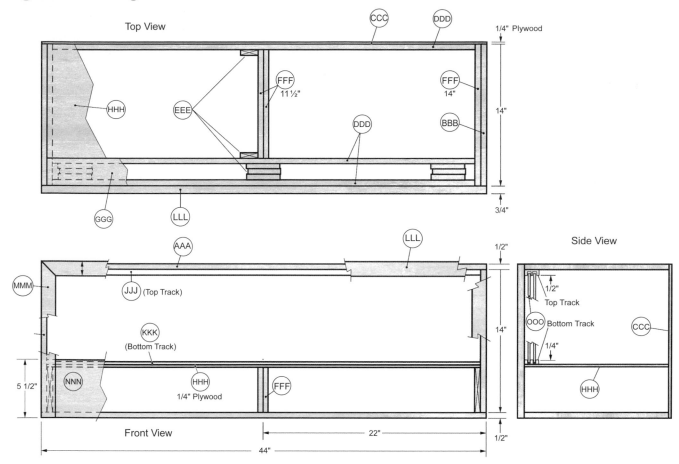

The final step of creating this beast is building and installing the drawers. Build the drawer boxes as shown in Photo 19. *Remember,* the finished drawer box should be about 1⅛" narrower than the opening to allow plenty of room for the drawer glides. Install the drawer glides, drawers and drawer faces (SS) as seen in Photo 20. For more information on installing drawers, see "The Fine Art of Installing Drawer Glides" in the Cube-Iture project (p. 37).

Build the Sliding Door Cabinet

The purpose of the sliding door cabinet is threefold: 1) It fills the 14" to 16" void the mattress doesn't fill in the upper bed area, 2) It provides a convenient place for setting alarm clocks, reading lights and other stuff,

Parts & Cutting List
(Upper Sliding Door Unit)

Part	Dimension	Qty
(AAA) Box top/ bottom	½" x 14" x 44"	2
(BBB) Box sides	½" x 14" x 14"	2
(CCC) Box back	¼" x 15" x 44"	1
(DDD) Long bottom supports	½" x 4⅝" x 43"	3
(EEE) Blocking	½" x 4⅝" x 3"	11
(FFF) Bottom supports	½" x 4⅝" x 11½" and 14"	4
(GGG) Narrow bottom strip	¼" x 2¼" x 43"	1
(HHH) Bottom panels	¼" x 11¾" x 21½"	2
(JJJ) Top door track	½" x 1⅛" x 43" *	1
(KKK) Bottom door track	¼" x 1⅛" x 43" *	1
(LLL) Top trim piece	¾" x 1¼" x 44" (mitered both ends)	1
(MMM) Side trim pieces	¾" x 1¼" x 15" (mitered one end)	2
(NNN) Bottom trim piece	¾" x 5½" x 41½"	1
(OOO) Sliding doors	¼" x 8¾' X 22"	2

Top (JJJ) and bottom (KKK) door tracks were purchased through Rockler Woodworking, rockler.com

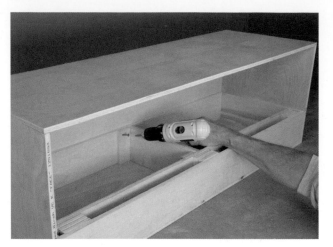

21 **BUILD** the sliding door cabinet. The multiple plywood supports and blocking pieces are used to support the panels for the hidden compartment.

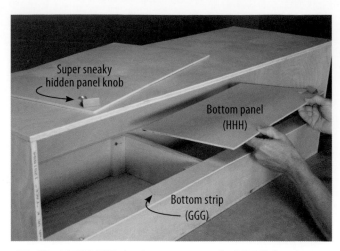

Super sneaky hidden panel knob

Bottom panel (HHH)

Bottom strip (GGG)

22 **TEST FIT** the bottom panels (HHH) for the hidden compartment. The binder clips serve as incognito knobs.

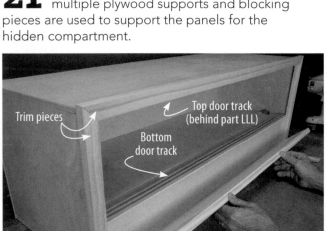

Trim pieces

Top door track (behind part LLL)

Bottom door track

Bottom trim (NNN)

23 **INSTALL** the trim pieces and top and bottom door tracks. The "deeper" of the two door tracks goes on top.

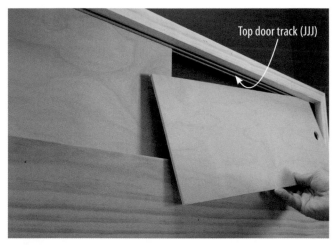

Top door track (JJJ)

24 **LIFT AND DROP** the door panels into the door tracks. Trim the height of the doors if necessary for easy installation and sliding.

3) It contains a hidden compartment for storing diaries and other treasures of youth.

Build the cabinet box as shown in Figure 4 and Photo 21. You can adjust the height and depth of the cabinet—but not the width since it needs to fit snuggly between the side panels of the bed itself. Install the bottom strip (GGG) near the front of the cabinet, then set the two bottom panels (HHH) in place as shown in Photo 22. The binder clips are "incognito knobs" used for removing the panels when accessing the compartment below. Choose your own secret knob and secure it with epoxy glue.

Add the top and bottom door tracks (the deep track mounts on top), then the trim pieces as shown in Photo 23. Finally install the sliding doors (OOO) by pushing them up into the upper track and letting them drop back down into the lower track.

"I Can Do Anything!" Mirror

Inspirational, fun and reflective

My wife, Kat, and I have a tradition of buying our six (soon to be more) granddaughters identical dresses every Christmas season and bringing them to the Minneapolis Children's Theatre. After the play one afternoon, a woman stopped us, "My you girls look wonderful! And I bet you're just as smart and beautiful on the inside as you are on the outside!" What a gift—to our granddaughters *and* to us—to have someone take the time to remind us of the truly important qualities.

So, I made this mirror to remind, not just my granddaughters, but other kids, who they are and what they can be. With a little luck, as they get up each morning and glance in the mirror to get ready for school, play and, even, work they'll remember they *can* do anything. Now *that's* something to reflect upon. We added a little height marking chart on the right side for kicks.

We provide the basic steps and measurements, but we encourage you to customize and personalize your mirror to suit the kid in your life.

How to Do It

Before you start, buy your mirror. We bought our 14" x 54" door mirror at a home center; big box retailers stock a variety of sizes, and glass specialty stores will cut one any size you want.

Cut the mirror backing (A) and mirror face (B) to size; they're identical in thickness, length and width. Position the mirror on the mirror back (Photo 1) and secure it with "mirror adhesive" (which won't corrode the silvering.) Surround it tightly with ⅛" Masonite or plywood—the same thickness as the mirror—and secure the strips with white glue.

Head to your computer. Fiddle around with the words you want to use and select a font and size that will work for your project. (We used "Footlight MT Light.") Find graphics you like, too. We downloaded ours from www.pixabay.com. You can also use photos from your own archives or buy decals online. Print your selections out on ordinary paper (Photo 2), cut them out and arrange them on your mirror face (Photo 3). As you lay things out, bear in mind the face plywood (B) needs to overlap the mirror edges by at least ½" on all sides.

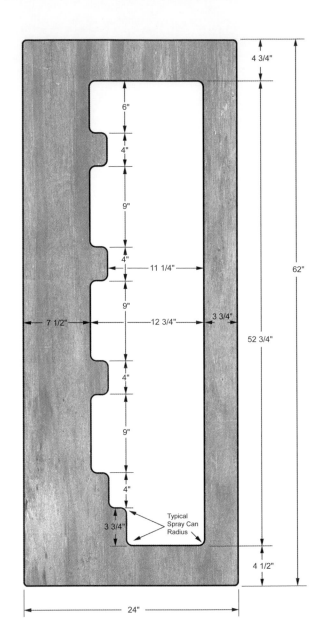

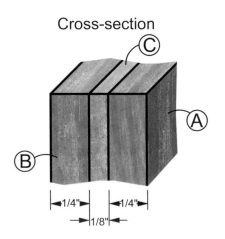

Cross-section

Cutting List

Part	Dimension	Qty
(A) Mirror back	¼" x 24" x 62" AC plywood	1
(B) Mirror face	¼" x 24" x 62" AC plywood	1
(C) Mirror surround	⅛" Masonite strips (cut to fit)	as needed

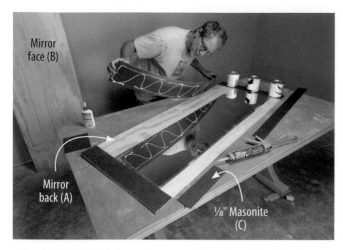

1 **POSITION** the mirror on the mirror back (A), holding it in place with dabs of mirror adhesive. Spread white glue on the backs of the ⅛" Masonite surround pieces (C) and use paint cans or other weights to "clamp" the pieces together.

2 **PRINT OUT** the words and graphics you plan to use on plain paper. Once you've fiddled with the design and layout (next photo), print the final versions on "clear sticker project" paper such as Avery #4397.

3 **LAYOUT** the positions of your words and graphics, then establish the shape of the mirror opening. You want the opening to overlap the edges of the mirror by at least ½" on all sides.

4 **CUT OUT** the opening using a jigsaw for the curves and circular saw for the long straightaways.

Make It Your Own

You can copy our design exactly—but it's way more fun to create your own mirror. Think about what you want your mirror to say and experiment with different fonts on your computer. To find graphics, type whatever you're looking for into your search engine followed by the words "scrap art" or "images." You'll find tons of stuff; most of it free.

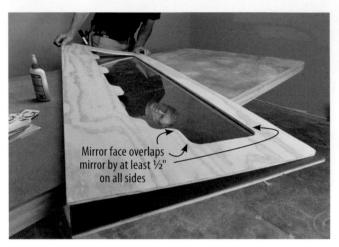

Mirror face overlaps mirror by at least ½" on all sides

5 **DRY** FIT the mirror face. If everything looks good, round over the edges, paint the surface and apply the stickers or decals.

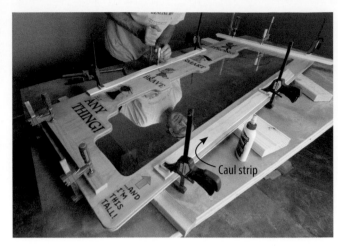

Caul strip

6 **GLUE** and clamp the mirror face in place. Use "caul strips" to help evenly distribute the pressure from the clamps.

Once your lettering, opening and graphics all jibe, print your graphics onto clear "sticker" paper available at office supply stores. Cut out the mirror opening as shown in Photo 4 and test fit the parts (Photo 5.) Sand or rout the edges, paint the face plywood then apply your graphics. Use white glue and clamps to secure the face (Photo 6).

Oops

When I was building the prototype for this mirror, I printed the images and words onto "sticker paper" (about $1/sheet) without first experimenting on plain paper (about 2 cents/sheet). Things just didn't look right and I wound up with $10 worth of very expensive scrap paper.

Nanny Rocker

Two can rock as easily as one

"Nanny Rockers," according to legend, were born in the deep south. They allowed caretakers to soothe newborns and carry on with their work at the same time. Multi-tasking is clearly not an invention of the Internet Age.

There are hardwood Nanny Rockers so beautifully crafted they could sit in the Decorative Arts section of the Louvre. But their joinery is so complex and parts so numerous, it takes a serious craftsman to tackle one of those. We've vastly simplified the process by using plywood for the sides and dowels for the spindles.

Build the Main Framework

The main structure of this rocker consists of a chair end panel (A), a cradle end panel (B) and a divider panel (C) which does double duty as cradle end and chair armrest. Your first step is to layout the chair end panel (A); in turn, you'll use this to lay out the other two panels as shown in Photo 3.

Begin laying out the chair end panel (A) by drawing the center-line (Photo 1), then using this line as a reference for laying out the other arcs and lines shown in Figure 1. Use your tape measure hooked on a screw as a gigantic compass to draw the curves. Once you have all the lines and arcs drawn, check and double check your layout lines; get this part right and the parts based on this (B,C) will be right too!

Cutting List

Part	Dimensions	Qty
(A) Rocking chair side panel	¾" x 40" x 42" plywood *	1
(B) Cradle side panel	¾" x 29" x 40" plywood *	1
(C) Divider panel	¾" x 30" x 24" plywood *	1
(D) Bottom supports	1⅛" x 3½" x 16" pine	2
(E) Stretchers	1⅛" x 3½" x 52" pine	2
(F) Bottom	¾" x 21" x 52" plywood	1
(G) Bottom cradle rail	1⅛" x 2" x 30¼" pine	2
(H) Top cradle rail	1⅛" x 1¼" x 30¼" pine	2
(J) Cradle spindles	¾" x 6½" pine	20
(K) Chair back bottom rail	1⅛" x 1½" x 21" pine	1
(L) Chair back top rail	1⅛" x 3½" x 21"	1
(M) Chair back spindles	½" x 15⅞" pine	6
(N) Chair armrests	¾" x 2" x 22" pine	2
(P) Rocker battens	½" x 1⅛" x 42" oak **	2
(Q) Magazine rack top	¾" x 3" x 12" ***	1
(R) Magazine rack bottom	¾" x 3" x 12" ***	1
(S) Magazine rack spindles	⅜" x 6½" pine	11

*Approximate size
**Cut to length after installed
***Cut to shape

Figure 1:
Side View

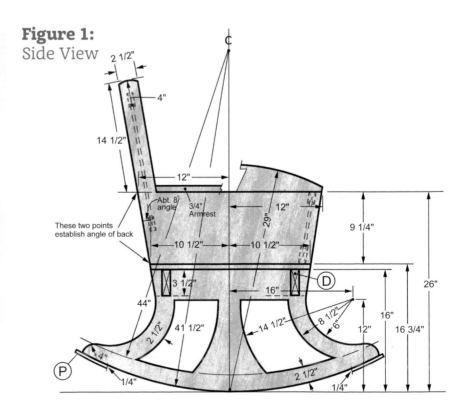

Figure 2: Front View

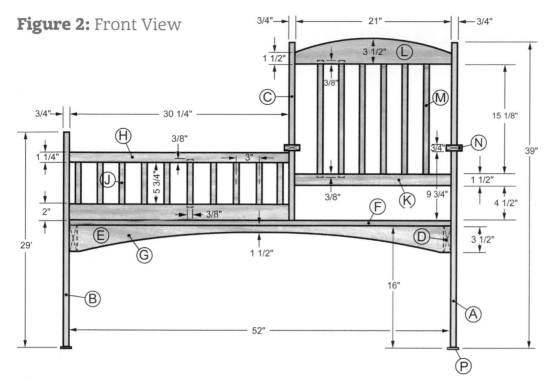

Figure 3: Top View

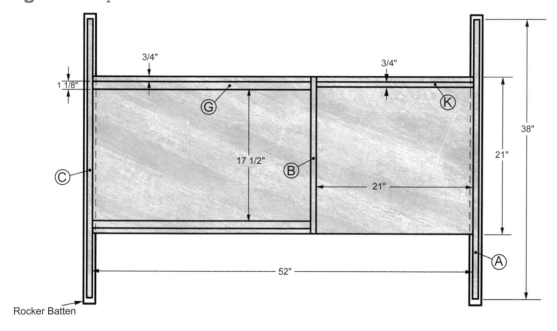

Rocker Batten

Materials List

Material	Qty
¾" x 4' x 8' birch, maple or other plywood	1
⁵⁄₄" x 4" x 8' pine	4
1 x 4 x 8' pine (armrests and mag rack)	1
½" x 1⅛" x 8' oak mull strip (for rocker battens)	1
¾" x 48" dowels	3
½" x 48" dowels	2

Ooops!

Once the rocker was built, I asked friends to "test drive" it. They universally loved the size, shape, design (and book nook), but a couple of people wondered if the fronts of the rockers couldn't be shortened to be less obtrusive. It would be easy to shorten them 4 inches without impacting stability—and I just might do that.

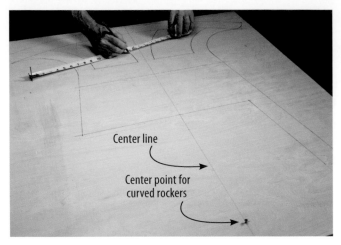

1 LAYOUT rocking chair panel (A) using the dimensions shown in Figure 1. Draw the large arcs using a screw as a center point and a tape measure as compass.

2 CUT the panel to shape. Use a circular saw for the long straight parts and a jigsaw for the curves. The starter holes create an entry point for the jigsaw blade and create nice round inside corners.

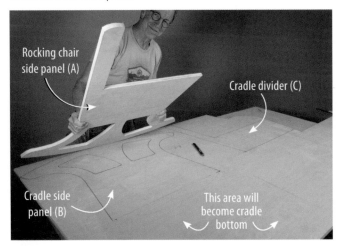

3 USE the rocking chair panel (A) as a template for laying out Parts B & C. The remaining section of plywood will become the cradle bottom (F).

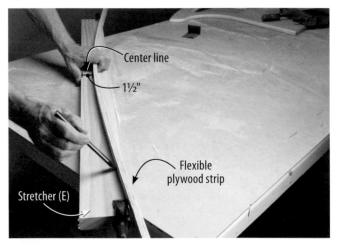

4 CREATE the curves in the stretchers (E) by bending a thin strip of plywood between a pair of clamps and tracing along the outer edge.

Use a circular saw to cut out the straight sections and a jigsaw for the curves (Photo 2). The 1-in. holes shown do double duty: They provide entry points for the jigsaw blade and produce nice, round inside corners in the cutout areas.

Next, make Parts B and C. As you can see in Photo 3, this good-looking fellow has traced around Part A to create the other two parts. Part B doesn't include the long skinny backrest part. But it does include an added arch on the top. Part C—the divider panel—consists of only the top part of the template. Take note that by laying out Parts A & B as

shown you'll get efficient use of the plywood; it leaves a long wide piece you can use for the bottom (F). Cut out Parts B and C, sand to remove any bumps or dips, then use a router with a ¼" round over bit to soften the edges.

Craft the two stretchers (E). Cut the boards to length, find the centers, then make a mark 1½" down from the top (Photo 4). Secure clamps near both ends of the boards, then push the center of a narrow strip of plywood up to your center mark and trace along the edge to create the curve.

Glue and screw the bottom supports (D) to Parts A and B as shown in Photo 5. Use clamps

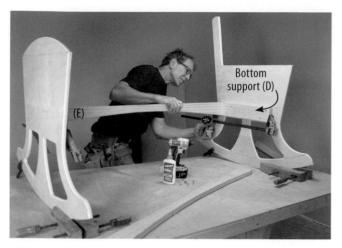

5 **INSTALL** the bottom supports (D) and stretchers (E) using glue and screws. Clamps offer a second pair of hands where needed.

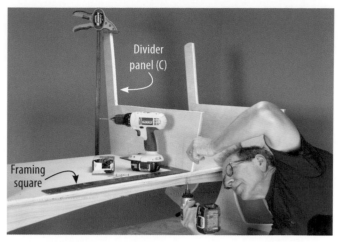

6 **SECURE** the divider panel (C) to the bottom with screws. Use a framing square to position the panel square with the front edge.

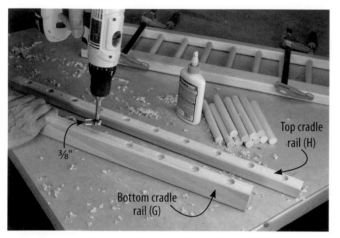

7 **BUILD** the crib side "ladders" by boring holes in the top and bottom rails, gluing the spindles in place, then applying clamps. Use the ⅜" depth of the drill bit cutter head as a guide for boring uniform ⅜" deep holes.

8 **SCREW** the crib sides in place. Use clamps to pull the cradle sides tightly against the rails during installation.

to hold the two end pieces upright and more clamps to hold the stretchers in place, then screw and glue the stretchers to the bottom supports. Cut the bottom (F) to size, round over the long edges, then use glue and screws to secure it to the stretchers and bottom supports. The bottom will overhang the stretchers by 1½".

Mark the position of the divider panel (C), use clamps to hold it in place, then secure it to the bottom using screws as shown in Photo 6. Predrill the holes for best results. Congratulations, the main framework of your rocker is complete.

Add the Spindles, Arms and Rocker Strips

To create the cradle sides (Photo 7), cut the top rails (H) and bottom rails (G) to length, then layout the centers of the spindle holes as shown in Figure 2. Use a ¾" Forstner bit to bore ⅜" deep holes.

Apply glue to the sides and bottom of the holes, slide the spindles into place, then use clamps to hold the rails and spindles together while the glue dries. Install the rails between the cradle sides (B,C) as shown in Photo 8. Build the back of the chair (K,L,M)

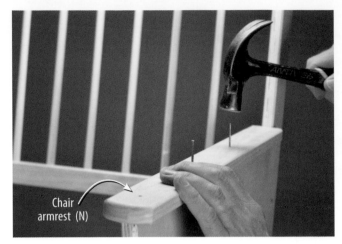

Chair armrest (N)

9 **GLUE** and screw the armrests (N) to the rocker side panels. Curve the front edge and use a round over bit to soften the edges before installation.

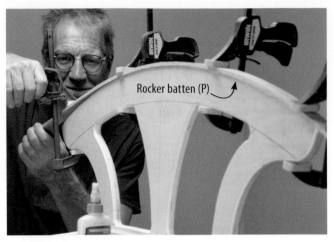

Rocker batten (P)

10 **APPLY** glue to the rocker battens (P), then use clamps and finish nails to secure them in place. Trim the strips to length once the glue is dry and clamps are removed.

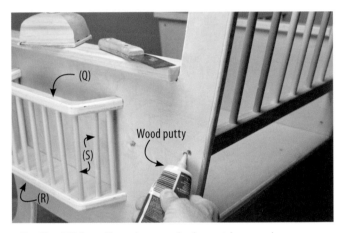

(Q)

(S)

(R)

Wood putty

11 **FILL** nail and screw holes with wood putty, then sand. Apply a clear finish or prime and paint.

Sweet Dreams ★ ★ ★

12 **APPLY** decals if you wish. The "reverse die cut" decal shown is self-sticking and relatively easy to install.

using the same procedure. Once the glue has dried, install the assembled back. Cut the armrests (N) to length, round over the edges, then glue and screw them to the flat tops of the chair sides (A, C) as shown in Photo 9.

Turn the rocker upside down, apply glue to the rocker battens (P), then use clamps and nails to secure them to the plywood rockers as shown in Photo 10.

Build the optional book nook (Q, R, S) and secure it to the side of the chair with screws and glue. Use sandable wood putty to fill screw and nail holes (Photo 11), then give the entire chair a sanding to remove dried glue or rough spots. Brush on a clear finish or apply a coat

QUICK TIP

Install rocker battens that are a few inches longer than needed; the overhanging area will give you a place to apply more clamps and, in turn, get better leverage at the ends where it's needed. Saw the battens to proper length once the glue has set.

of primer, followed by your color of choice. The "Sweet Dreams" and stars (Photo 12) are "reverse die cut" decals available through Amazon.com, Etsy.com and other sources.

Install a crib mattress (see "Build it Safe"), add a chair cushion and rock that newborn—and maybe yourself—to sleep.

Portable Desk

A mini-work station for artists, writers and inventors

Lap desk, floor easel, art suitcase—call it what you will, this little take along
is multi-talented.

- The slanted top serves as an easel for drawing.
- The PVC pencil holder keeps the lid propped up at a comfortable angle
  for use as an upright easel. Remove the pencil holder and open the
  lid all the way to create a flat surface for writing or building.
- The innards are large enough to store loads of art supplies.
- The short legs raise it far enough so it can comfortably be used on the
  floor, while seated or even in bed.
- It's got a handle for hauling it around and magnetic clasp for keeping it shut.

Figure 1

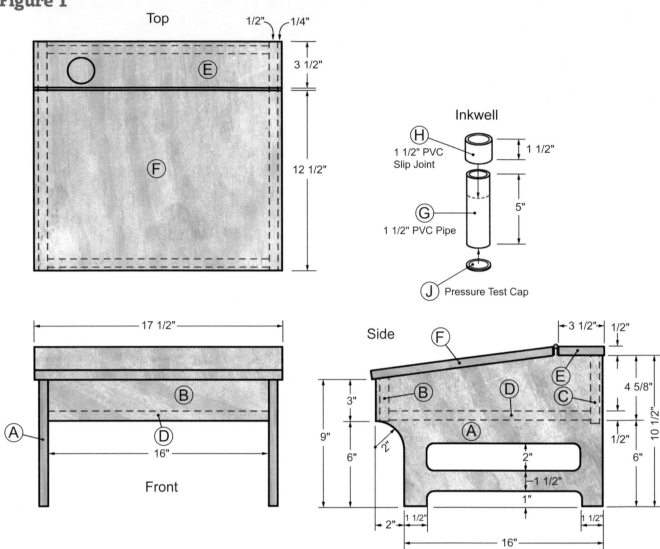

Cutting List

Part	Dimensions	Qty
(A) Side	½" x 10½" x 16" birch plywood	2
(B) Front	½" x 3" x 16" birch plywood	1
(C) Back	½" x 4⅝" x 16" birch plywood	1
(D) Bottom	½" x 14¾" x 16" birch plywood	1
(E) Lid support	½" x 3¾" x 17½" birch ply	1
(F) Lid	½" x 12½" x 17½" birch ply	1
(G) Inkwell	1½" x 5" PVC pipe	1
(H) Inkwell collar	1½" x PVC slip joint	1
(J) Inkwell bottom	1½" pressure test cap	1

Materials List

Material	Qty
½" x 4' x 4' birch plywood	1
16" piano hinge	1
PVC pipe and fittings, magnetic catch, handle	

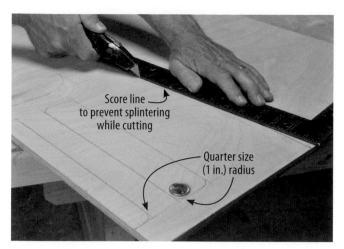

1 **LAYOUT** one side based on Figure 1. Score the lines with a utility knife—then cut just outside the line—to minimize splintering when cutting.

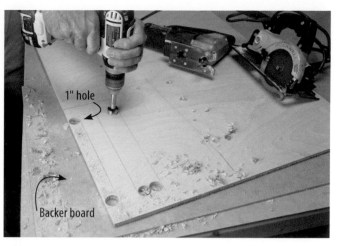

2 **BORE** 1" holes to create uniform corners. The backer board prevents splintering when the drill exits the back side.

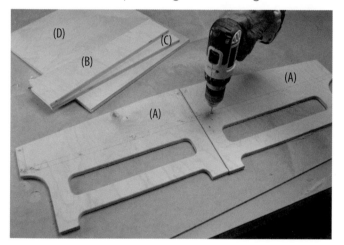

3 **DRILL** pilot holes for the nails securing the front, back and bottom. Arrange your sides "butterfly style" to ensure you're laying out one left and one right side.

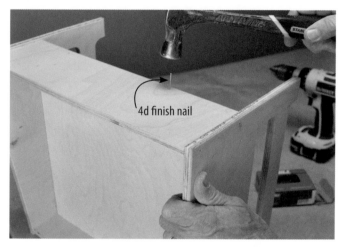

4 **ASSEMBLE** the basic box using white glue and 4d finish nails. Install the piano hinge that secures the lid support (E) to the lid (F), then secure that to the back of the box.

How to Build It

Start by laying out one of the sides (A) as shown in Photo 1. Use a 1-inch drill bit to "cut" the inside corners of the cutout and leg areas (Photo 2). Use a jigsaw and circular saw to cut the first side to shape, then use that as a pattern for the other side. Use a router with a ¼" round over bit to soften the edges.

Position the sides as mirror images (Photo 3) then draw in the positions of the front (B), back (C) and bottom (D) panels. Drill pilot holes as shown, then use glue and 4d finish nails to secure the parts together to create the basic box (Photo 4).

Attach the lid support (E) to the lid (F) with a 16" piano hinge; use the narrow hinges—each leaf is usually ½" wide—for

> **QUICK TIP**
>
> *To prevent splintering on the top side when cutting, score through the top veneer layer with a utility knife as shown in Photo 1, then cut just outside the line.*

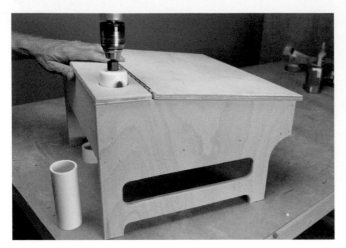

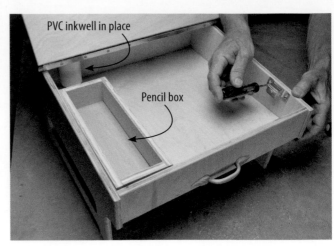

PVC inkwell in place

Pencil box

5 **CREATE** a hole for the PVC inkwell using a 2" hole saw. The inkwell provides pencil storage and helps prop the lid at the right angle when open.

6 **INSTALL** the magnetic catch to keep the lid closed when the desk is being carried by the handle.

the best fit. Secure the lid support to the top of the box using glue and 4d finish nails.

Bore a 2" hole for the "inkwell" (Photo 5). The inkwell is optional, but not only provides a place to store pens and pencils but also supports the lid, when open, at a slight angle. Glue the

inkwell parts (G, H, J) together and slip it in the hole. Finally install the metal catch and handle (Photo 6). If you need a pencil box, like you see to the side, bang one together from scraps.

Puppet Stage & Store Front

All the world's a stage...
or lemonade stand...or library

We hesitated giving this project a name because it can be used for so many things: Kool Aid stand, puppet stage, library, storefront, you name it. To keep it fun and flexible, the marquee, top and front panel are painted with chalkboard paint so kids can freely change their gig of choice.

Figure 1: Top View

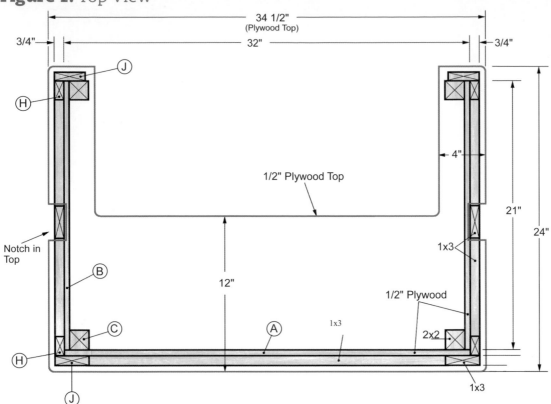

34 1/2" (Plywood Top)

3/4" — 32" — 3/4"

1/2" Plywood Top

4"

21"

24"

Notch in Top

12"

1x3

1/2" Plywood

2x2

1x3

(J) (H) (B) (C) (A) 1x3

Cutting List

Part	Dimension	Qty
(A) Front panel	½" x 24" x 32" ply	1
(B) Side panels	½" x 24" x 21" ply	2
(C) Corner posts	1½" x 1½" x 24"	4
(D) Side bottom batten	¾" x 2½" x 21½"	2
(E) Front top & bottom batten	¾" x 2½" x 33½"	2
(F) Sign posts	¾" x 2½" x 60"	2
(G) Side top battens	¾" x 2½" x 9½"	4
(H) Side corner battens	¾" x 1½" x 19"	4
(J) Front & Back corner battens	¾" x 2½" x 19"	4
(K) Top	½" x 24" x 34½"	1
(L) Marquee sign	½" x 10½" x 35"	1
(M) Bun feet	2" x 3" (diameter)	4

Materials List

Material	Qty
½" x 4' x 8' AC or better plywood	1
2 x 2 x 8' pine	1
1 x 3 x 8' pine	4
1 x 2 x 8' pine	1
2" x 3" bun feet	4

Figure 2: Side View

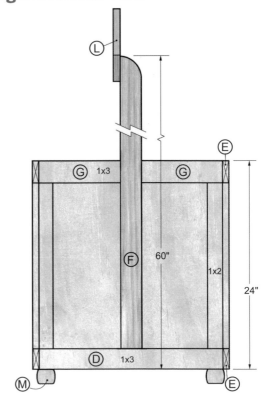

(L)

(E)

(G) 1x3   (G)

(F)

60"

1x2

24"

(D) 1x3

(M)   (E)

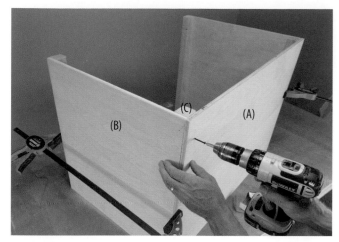

1 **BUILD** the basic box, using 2x2s and plywood. Keep screws close to the edges so the battens—installed later—will cover them.

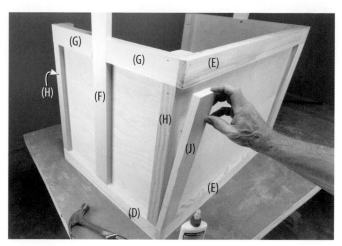

2 **GLUE** and nail the horizontal and vertical battens to the box in the alphabetical order shown.

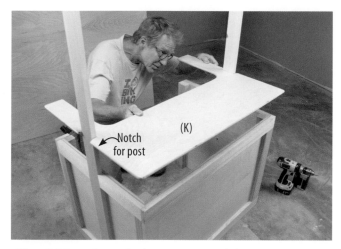

Notch for post

3 **CUT** and test fit the top. Round the corners and soften the edges. Leave the top loose for now so it can be removed for painting.

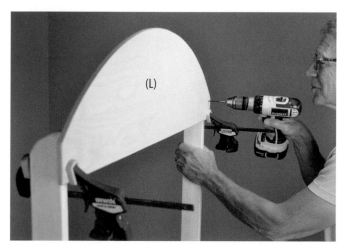

4 **INSTALL** the marquee. If you plan to paint it with chalkboard paint only use a couple of screws for now so it can be easily removed.

How to Build It

Secure the ends of the side panels (B) to the corner posts (C), then stand them up and screw the front panel (A) in place (Photo 1). Use clamps to hold the parts tight and square while you work.

Add the battens—in the alphabetical order shown in Photo 2—using glue and 6d finish nails. Use sandpaper to soften the edges and corners. Cut out the plywood top (K), leaving notches for the sign posts (F). Use a router and ¼" round over bit to soften the edges. Leave the top loose for now if you plan on painting it.

Better Yet

Add a shelf lengthwise inside the box. It adds stability to the legs and gives kids a place to store puppets or extra "stock" when selling lemonade.

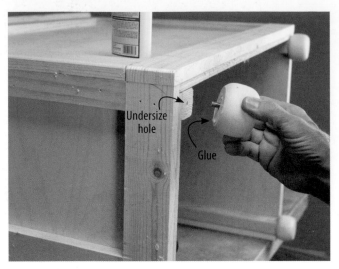

5 **ADD** the bun feet. These are designed to screw into metal brackets, but install them by applying glue and twisting them into slightly undersized holes.

Cut the marquee sign (L), round over the edges then use clamps to hold it in place while test fitting it. There's nothing sacred about the size and shape of the sign—have some fun with it. Finally, install the bun feet (Photo 5).

We painted the front panel (A), top (K) and marquee (L) with chalkboard paint. It required priming the boards, applying two coats of chalkboard paint, letting the paint cure for several days then "seasoning" it with chalk before using it. We used green Rustoleum Chalk Board paint, available at most home centers. Another option is whiteboard paint.

Puzzle Desk

A fun solution to a puzzling problem

Our daughter Kellie—starting at the age of three and still going strong—
has always loved jigsaw puzzles. Cookie Monster puzzles, Paris street scenes,
even those weird circular ones that are all white—she'd tackle 'em all. And
one puzzling thing we discovered about our puzzle put-er together-er was
she didn't have a good place to safely store her works in progress.

This desk takes a shot at solving the riddle. The drawers can be flipped upside
down to create flat puzzle-building surfaces; ones that—with the puzzle intact—
can be slid into the desk and out of the way. Right side up the drawers can be
used for storing boxed puzzles. And, of course the desk—along with the matching

Figure 1

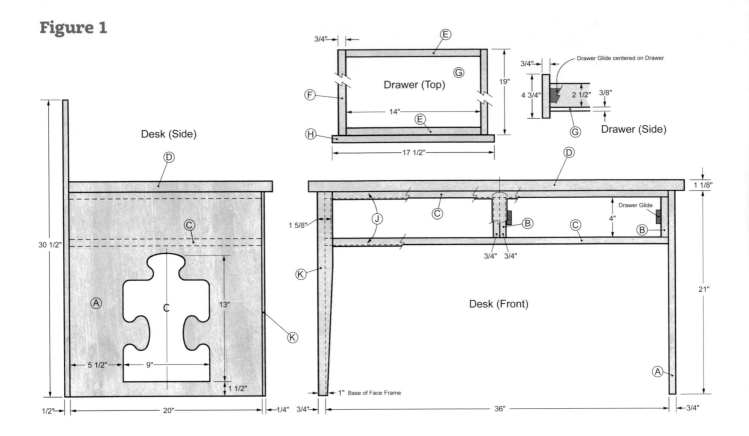

Cutting List

Part	Dimensions	Qty
(A) Leg panels	¾" x 20" x 21" plywood	2
(B) Drawer box verticals	¾" x 4" x 20" plywood	4
(C) Drawer box top & bottom	¾" x 20" x 36" plywood	2
(D) Desk top	1⅛" x 21" x 39" pine	1
(E) Drawer front/back	¾" x 2½" x 14" pine	4
(F) Drawer sides	¾" x 2½" x 19" pine	4
(G) Drawer bottom	⅜" x 15½" x 19" pine	2
(H) Drawer face	¾" x 4¾" x 17½" pine	2
(J) Horizontal face frame	¼" x ¾" x 34½"	2
(K) Leg face frame	¼" x 1⅝" x 21" *	2
(L) Center face frame	¼" x 1⅝" x 4"	1
(M) Back panel	⅜" x 30½" x 37½"	1

* *Taper cut (see diagram)*

Materials List

Material	Qty
⅜" x 4' x 4' AC plywood	1
¾" x 4' x 8' AC plywood	1
1 x 3 x 12' pine	1
1 x 6 x 4' pine	1
⁵⁄₄" x 21" x 48" glued-up pine panel	1
¼" x 2" x 10' pine mull strip	1
18" drawer glides	2 pair

Raise That Desk as Your Kids Grow Up

As kids grow taller, it's easy to raise the level of the desk three or four inches by adding bun feet or short legs to the bottom of the desk. You can find a wide variety of options at www.adamswoodproducts.com

1 **CUT** the leg panels to size using either a straight cutting jig as shown or a table saw. Cut the puzzle piece shape of your choosing into the side.

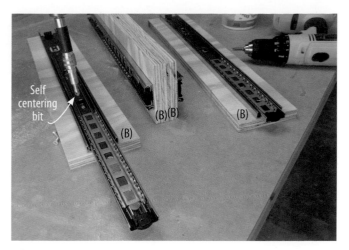

2 **SCREW** the sliding part of the drawer glides to the drawer box verticals (B). The self-centering bit helps drill precise pilot holes which in turn helps keep the glides centered.

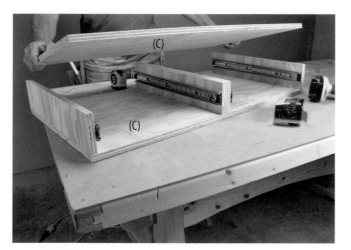

3 **BUILD** the drawer box. Make the drawer openings identical so the drawers can be interchanged and flip-flopped down the road.

4 **SECURE** the legs to the drawer box, making sure the tops of the legs are flush with the top of the box. Attach the top (D) to the box with drywall screws.

stools on the following pages—can be easily used as a "normal" workspace.

Note: While the drawers are designed to be used right side up and upside down, flipping the drawers around TOO much can add wear and tear to the mechanical drawer glides. Flip judiciously!

How to Build It

This desk is basically a "drawer box" suspended between two legs (A) with a back (M) and top (D) attached. Begin by cutting the two leg panels to size with either a table saw or

straight cutting jig (Photo 1). Cut the puzzle shaped openings and round over the edges. We don't give dimensions for the puzzle-shaped cutout—have fun designing your own; just make sure the top of the cutout extends no more than 15" from the bottom of the panel (or the drawer box will show through).

Next, cut the four drawer box verticals (B) and the drawer box top and bottom (C) to size. Secure the sliding part of the drawer glides to the centers of the verticals (B) as shown in Photo 2. It's way easier to do this now than after the box is assembled. Assemble the box (Photo 3).

5 **INSTALL** the drawer glides, making sure they're centered. See "The Fine Art of Installing Drawer Glides" on p. 37 for more information.

6 **NAIL** the back (M) to the legs and drawer box. The squareness of the back panel will help you "square up" the entire desk and add rigidity.

7 **GLUE** and nail the face frame members (J,K,L) to the fronts of the legs and drawer box to create a more finished look. Secure with 1" brads.

8 **SCREW** the drawer faces (H) to the drawer fronts. Drill oversize holes in the drawer itself so the front can be slightly adjusted.

Position your drawer box upside down on a flat surface (Photo 4), then secure the sides (A) using white glue and coarse drywall screws. Screw the top (D) in place using drywall screws driven up through the front opening and from the back.

Next, build the drawers (E, F, G), based on the diagram and cutting list. Install the glides to the drawer sides. Make sure to center the glide exactly; that way you can flip the drawer over to create the flat puzzle surface when needed.

Cut out and install the back (Photo 6); again, there's nothing set in stone about the puzzle shapes so have some fun with it. Glue and nail

the face frame pieces (J, K, L) to the front of the desk as shown in Photo 7. Note that the face frame members (K) for the legs are tapered.

Install the drawer fronts as shown in Photo 8. The holes in the front of the drawer are oversize so the front can be slightly adjusted as needed. Paint 'er up—have fun with that too—then start puzzling away.

Picture-Perfect Plywood

Well over half of the projects in this book use plywood in their construction—and for good reasons.

Plywood replaces complex joinery. Take Riley's Rocker (p. 105) as an example. The chair could have been made from solid wood, but it would have involved gluing up boards for the seat and back, bending wood for the rockers, creating individual spindles for the sides, then figuring out how to join all the parts together. Plywood eliminates most of these tasks—and still yields an attractive, functional piece of furniture.

It's inexpensive and widely available. Every home center and lumberyard on the planet carries pine plywood—and many carry birch, maple and oak as well.

It can be cut and shaped with everyday hand tools. If you have a circular saw, jigsaw and drill you're halfway home.

True, it can be a pain to haul—but remember, most home centers and lumberyards will give you a couple of free cuts with the purchase of a sheet.

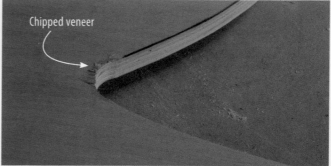

Chipped veneer

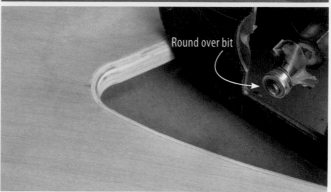

Round over bit

Score a line & cut good side down, especially with oak and other hardwood plywood. Circular saw blades and jigsaw blades cut on the upstroke (or up spin). This means they're pushing the thin veneer against the core on the bottom of the sheet but pushing it away at the top. This translates into more chipping on the top. To minimize top splintering, use a razor knife to score the cutline, then cut just outside of the line. The score line will limit splintering.

Round over edges (for lots of reasons). I nearly always soften or round over plywood edges with my router and a ¼" ball-bearing guided round over bit. This produces multiple benefits: 1) It gets rid of rough and chipped edges, 2) it makes dips and irregularities less obvious, 3) it creates a more paint-friendly edge, 4) it makes the corners more "touch friendly" and less likely to scrape little shins and chins.

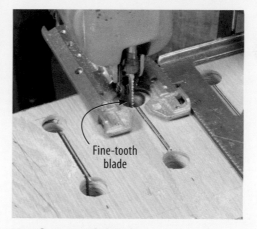

Fine-tooth blade

Use fine-tooth blades in your power saws. I keep a 60-tooth blade in my circular saw, an 80-tooth blade in my table saw and a 20-tooth-per-inch metal cutting blade in my jigsaw. They cut slower than blades with fewer teeth—but make up for lost time by creating cleaner cuts that require less sanding.

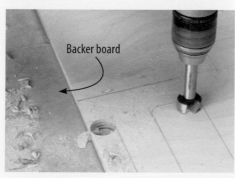

Backer board

(left) **Use a backer board** when drilling holes. Drill bits—especially spade or paddle bits—will "blow out" the veneer grain when they exit the backside of a sheet of plywood. Use a scrap piece of lumber or plywood to support the backside to prevent splintering.

Puzzle Stools

Mobile, interlocking and fun

It's no coincidence these puzzle stools are just the right size to fit the puzzle desk. But even if you build these stools independently, they're a fun addition to a playroom. The cubical stools interlock to create a bench and the tops open so you can store toys, books and other goodies within. And, hmm, with casters who could resist an indoor scooter stool?

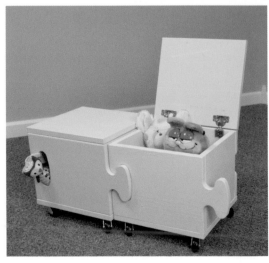

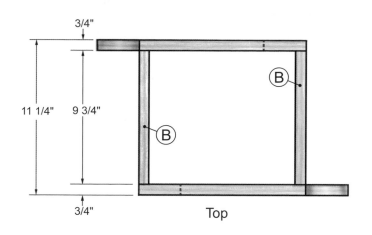

3/4"

11 1/4"   9 3/4"

3/4"

(B)

(B)

Top

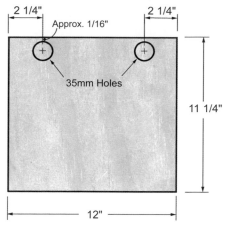

2 1/4"   2 1/4"

Approx. 1/16"

35mm Holes

11 1/4"

12"

Top (C) & Bottom (D)

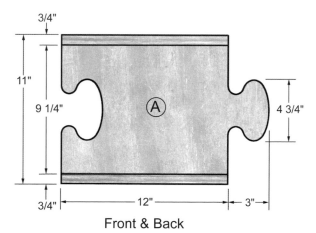

3/4"

11"

9 1/4"

(A)

4 3/4"

3/4"   12"   3"

Front & Back

Cutting List

Part	Dimensions	Qty
(A) Front/ back	1 x 10 x 15"	2
(B) Side	1 x 10 x 9¾"	2
(C) Bottom	1 x 11¼" x 12"	1
(D) Top	1 x 11¼" x 12"	1

Materials List (for two stools)

Material	Qty
1 x 10 x 10'	1
1 x 12 x 4'	1
2" casters	8
"Full overlay" cup hinges	4

How to Build It

Start by tracing the puzzle shape (page 95) onto the 1x10 you'll use for the fronts and backs (A). You can "nest cut" them as shown in Photo 1 to minimize waste and the amount of cutting you need to do—but if the curves are too tight for you or your saw, cut them out of individual 15" long pieces.

Sand the curved cutouts as shown in Photo 2. Remove at least ⅛" of material from all the curved edges of the tongues and indents so the parts will easily interlock when you hook the individual stools together. Use a router with a ¼" round over bit to soften all the edges. Use glue and trim head drywall screws to construct the boxes (Photo 3). Predrill the holes to prevent splitting.

Install the "full overlay" cup hinges shown in Photos 4 and 5. Begin by drilling a pair of 35 mm holes in the top boards (D). The instructions that come with the hinge will give you the precise distance the edge of the hole needs to be from the edge of the board; in our case, ¹⁄₁₆". Insert the cup portion of the hinge into the hole and secure it with two screws. Secure the other leaf of the hinge to the inside of the box as shown in Photo 5. The adjustment screws built into the hinge allow you to align the top and box after the hinges have been installed.

Install the casters as shown in Photo 6. If you have thick carpet or need to raise the height of the stools, install taller or larger casters.

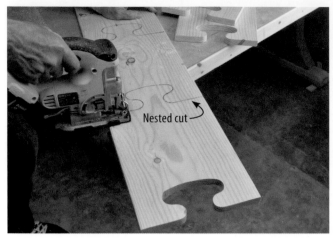

1 CUT OUT the puzzle-shape front and back panels. Use a thin jigsaw blade with coarse teeth to negotiate the tight curves.

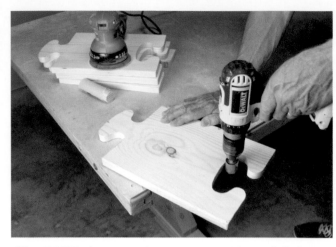

2 SAND the curved cutout areas. Use a drill drum sander or 1" dowel with sandpaper wrapped around it. Round over the edges with a router.

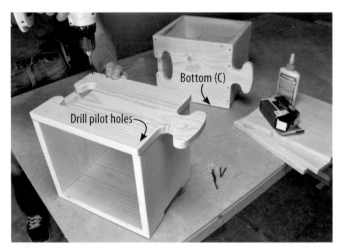

3 SCREW the basic box together using glue and trim head drywall screws, then install the bottom (C).

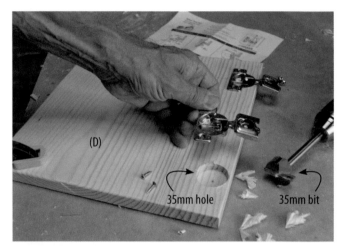

4 INSTALL the euro-style cup hinges in 35 mm holes bored in the top. The hinge directions will stipulate how far from the edge the hole should be.

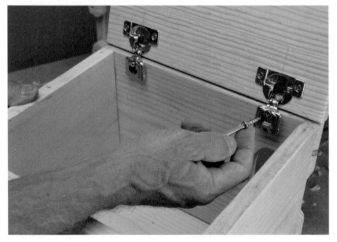

5 SECURE the other leaf of the hinge to the inside of the box.

6 INSTALL the four casters. If you'll be rolling over rough terrain (like thick carpet) or you need more height, install larger casters.

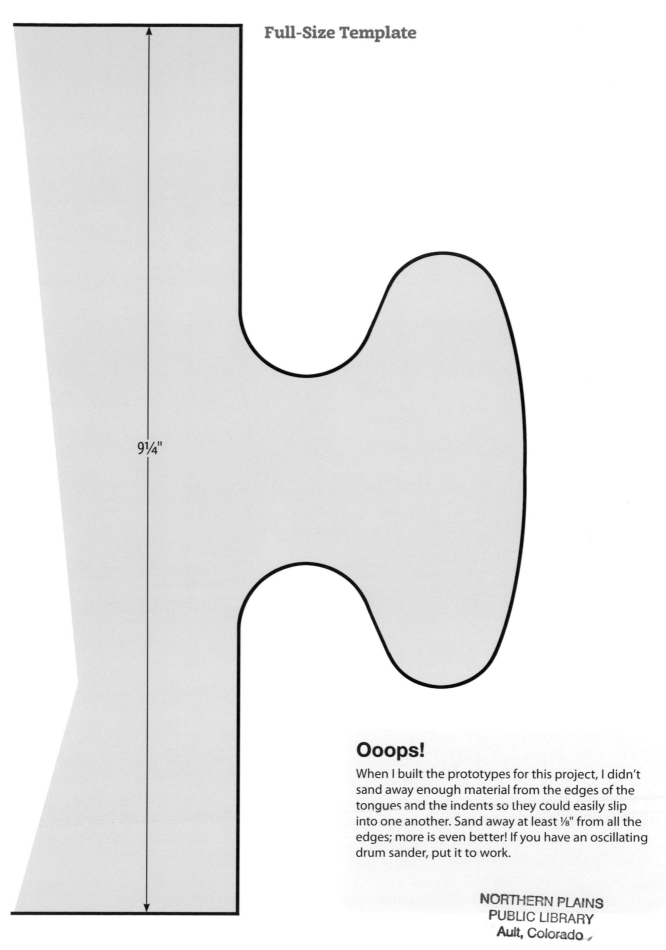

Full-Size Template

9¼"

Ooops!

When I built the prototypes for this project, I didn't sand away enough material from the edges of the tongues and the indents so they could easily slip into one another. Sand away at least ⅛" from all the edges; more is even better! If you have an oscillating drum sander, put it to work.

PVC Teepee

A cozy hideaway you can make with your kids

My favorite hangout when I was a kid was my Davy Crockett tent. I'd pitch it indoors and out; use it spring, summer and fall; play in it by day and (when I was lucky) sleep in it by night. There was something special and "mine" about it.

Here's a special hideaway you can build with your kids. It's made from inexpensive PVC pipe and fittings, and a painters' tarp. You can build it in an afternoon, your kids will have fun building and it's easy to take apart for storage.

Figure 1: Pipe Detail

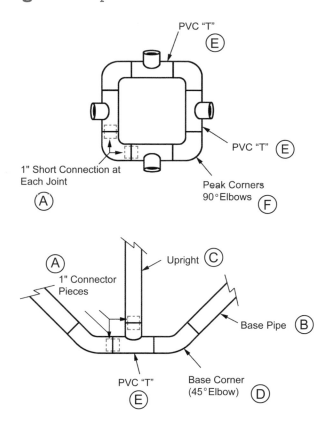

PVC "T" Ⓔ

PVC "T" Ⓔ

1" Short Connection at Each Joint Ⓐ

Peak Corners 90° Elbows Ⓕ

Upright Ⓒ

Ⓐ 1" Connector Pieces

Base Pipe Ⓑ

PVC "T" Ⓔ

Base Corner (45° Elbow) Ⓓ

Figure 2: Canvas

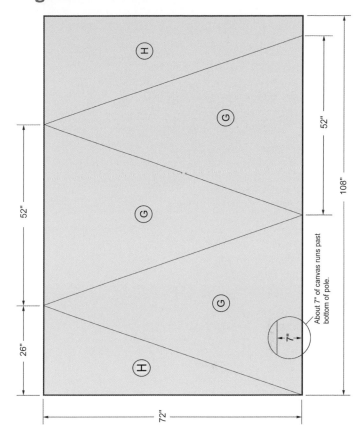

Ⓗ

Ⓖ

Ⓖ

Ⓖ

Ⓖ

Ⓗ

52"

108"

52"

26"

72"

About 7" of canvas runs past bottom of pole.

7"

How to Do It

Start by cutting the pipe to length (Photo 1). Cut the long sections (B,C) first, then use the scraps for the short connectors (A). We show a Japanese pull saw, but any fine-tooth saw will work. If a kid is cutting, make sure to clamp the pipe securely so they can keep both hands on the saw and focus on sawing. The hand screw clamp holds the pipe, establishes the right length and provides a square surface for guiding the saw.

Pre-assemble the peak and the four base corner assemblies (Photo 2). There's no need to use glue; friction will do the job. Assemble the square base using the four base pipes (B) and four corner assemblies. Insert the four vertical uprights (C) into the peak assembly (Photo 3), then insert the free ends into the base corners. You'll have to twist the assemblies around a little to make everything align.

Cutting List

Part	Dimension	Qty
(A) Short connectors	½" x 1" PVC	16
(B) Base pipe	½" x 40" PVC	4
(C) Uprights	½" x 60" PVC	4
(D) Base Corners	½" x 45-degree elbows	8
(E) Base & peak "T"s	½" PVC Tees	8
(F) Peak Corners	½" x 90-degree elbows	4
(G) Full canvas triangle	52" x 72" tall triangle	3
(H) Half canvas triangle	varies x 72" tall	2

Materials List

Part	Qty
½" x 10' PVC pipe	4
½" x 45-degree elbows	8
½" x 90-degree elbows	4
½" PVC "T"s	8
6' x 9' canvas painter tarp	1
½" "RMC" conduit clamps	about 20

1 **CUT** the PVC pipe to length starting with the longest pieces, then use the cutoffs for the sixteen 1" connectors (A).

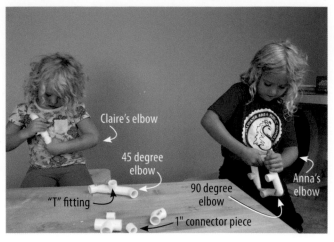

2 **ASSEMBLE** the peak and the four corner assemblies. No need to use glue; friction will work well enough.

3 **BUILD** the teepee framework. Adjust the angles of the "T"s at the corners and peaks so the uprights (C) form a symmetrical pyramid.

Lay a 6' x 9' canvas painter's tarp on the floor and mark it out (Photo 4) as shown in the diagram. Use a sturdy scissors to cut the canvas into triangles; you'll wind up with three full triangles (G) and two half panels (H) that will serve as the door. Secure the triangles to one another by overlapping the edges one inch and sealing them with hot melt glue (Photo 5). Turn your kids loose with their paint brushes. The tent cover will look like a colorful ½ pie when you're done (Photo 6).

Loosely drape the tent covering over the frame and adjust it, starting at the bottom, until the seams fall generally over the uprights. You'll have about 6" of excess material at the bottom, which you can fold under and secure with clips. You'll have a little excess at the top, too. Use ½" "RMC" galvanized conduit clamps (the ½" "EMT" ones are too small) with the ends bent over, to snap the tent covering to the frame.

Inspector

52"

72"

4 (left) **DRAW OUT** the triangles on the painter's canvas using the measurements in the diagram, then cut with a sharp sturdy scissors. A standard 6' x 9' tarp works perfectly.

5 (below) **OVERLAP** the edge of one triangle onto another by about 1-in, then in short increments use hot melt glue to join the edges.

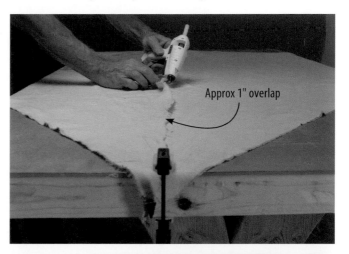

Approx 1" overlap

6 **SPREAD** the tent cover flat and paint the panels.

7 **SECURE** the canvas to the PVC pipe framework with ½" RMC conduit clips. Use a needle nose pliers to bend the ears back before installing them.

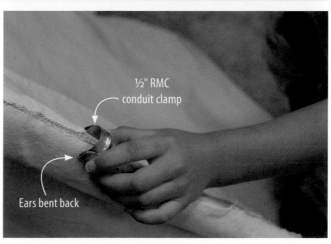

½" RMC conduit clamp

Ears bent back

Pyramid Picnic Table

A new angle on an outdoor table

There are a thousand plans for kids' picnic tables out there—and 999 of them have A-shaped legs with a rectangular top and two long seats.

If you're looking for something more unique, more compact, and less tippy—yet easy to build—check out this one. The footprint is a mere 4' x 4', yet there's plenty of room for friends to gather, play and eat. You can build it in an afternoon and when you're done, you'll be an expert at cutting 45-degree angles.

Figure 1: Leg with Seat Support

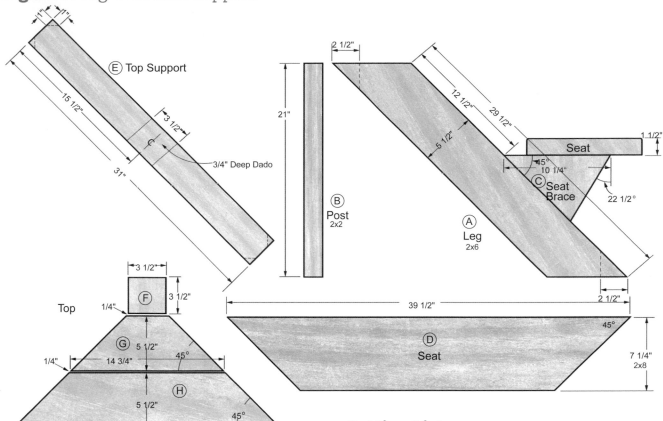

How to Do It

Round up your tools and lumber. We used treated lumber for the framework, legs and seats because of its low cost and high strength. If you use treated wood for the table top, cover it with a tablecloth when food is served, just to play it safe. Another option is to use composite, cedar or other exterior wood for the top boards.

Cut the four legs as shown in Photo 1 and Diagram A. Take your time to accurately lay out and cut one leg, then use that as a pattern for the other three. Lay the temporary post (B) flat on your work surface and secure two opposing legs to the top using 3" screws. Stand up this assembly and install the other two legs to create a pyramid shape. (Photo 2.)

Cut your four 2x8 seat boards to the dimensions shown and set them aside. Use the angled end cutoffs (Photo 3) to create the four seat braces (C). Make layout marks 12½" from

Cutting List

Part	Dimension	Qty
(A) Leg	2 x 6 x 29½" (45° angles)	4
(B) Post	2 x 2 x 21"	1
(C) Seat brace	2 x 10¼" (45° and 22½° angles)	4
(D) Seat	2 x 8 x 39½" (45° angles)	4
(E) Top support	2 x 4 x 31"	2
(F) Top board	⁵⁄₄" x 3½" x 3½"	1
(G) Top board	⁵⁄₄" x 5½" x 14¾" (45° angles)	4
(H) Top board	⁵⁄₄" x 5½" x 26¼" (45° angles)	4

Materials List

Material	Qty
(All material is treated lumber)	
2" x 2" x 24"	1
2" x 4" x 6'	1
2" x 6" x 10'	1
2" x 8" x 8'	2
⁵⁄₄" x 5½" x 12'	1
2½" ext screws	1 lb.
3" ext. screws	1 lb.
Constr Adhesive	1 tube

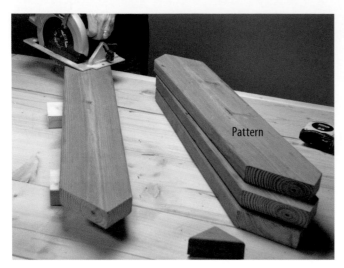

1 **CUT** the four legs (A) using the measurements and angles in Figure 1. For speed and accuracy, cut out one leg, then use that as a pattern for the other three.

2 **SECURE** the legs to the center post (B) using deck screws. **Note**: Once the seat and top boards are installed, you'll saw off the bottom part of the 2x2.

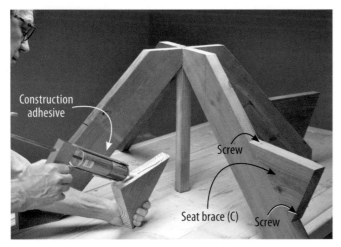

3 **GLUE** and screw the seat braces (C) to the legs as shown. The supports are made from end cuts from the 2x8 seat boards.

4 **POSITION** the 2x8 seat boards (D) and tweak the positions of the legs so the ends break on the centers of the braces. When everything aligns, predrill holes and screw the seats to the braces.

the tops of the legs, then secure the braces below these marks using construction adhesive and screws driven in from both the top and bottom.

Position your seat boards (D) and arrange them so they create a square and the ends are centered on the seat braces. You'll need to tweak the leg positions a little to get the ends of the seat boards to align right. When everything fits right, predrill holes in the ends of the seat boards and screw them down.

Cut the two top supports (E) to length, mark the centers, then measure 1¾" in each

direction to establish a pair of lines 3½" apart (the width of a 2x4.) Set your saw to cut ¾" deep, then make a series of cuts spaced about ½" apart (photo 5). Use your chisel to snap out these "fingers" then use the chisel, lying flat, to smooth the bottoms of the dados. Slide a scrap 1x4 into the dados to test the width and depth; it should nestle just right into the space.

Center one of the top supports, dado-side-up, over the legs (photo 6) and screw it in place, then secure the other one, dado-side-down as shown. Your "X" should have

5 **CUT** dadoes through the top supports (E) by making a series of ¾" cuts and removing the waste by prying out the "fingers." Use the chisel to flatten the bottoms of the dadoes.

6 **SCREW** one top support to the legs dado-side up, then secure the other one on top of it, dado-side down.

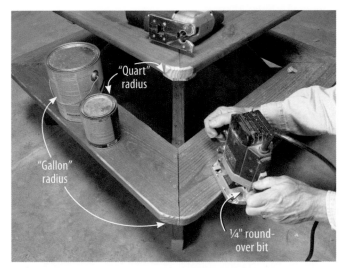

7 **SECURE** the top boards to the top supports, pre-drilling holes so the ends don't split when screws are driven.

8 **TRACE** around paint cans to establish the rounded corners, then cut them to shape with a jigsaw and soften the edges with a round-over router bit.

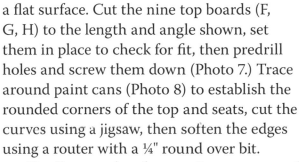

a flat surface. Cut the nine top boards (F, G, H) to the length and angle shown, set them in place to check for fit, then predrill holes and screw them down (Photo 7.) Trace around paint cans (Photo 8) to establish the rounded corners of the top and seats, cut the curves using a jigsaw, then soften the edges using a router with a ¼" round over bit.

Finally, use a handsaw or jig saw to cut off the lower portion of the center post (B) so it isn't in the way. Apply a coat of exterior stain or clear finish and break out the P, B and J.

Super-Duper Straight-Cutting Jig

A straight-cutting jig is a tool everyone should have; it's easy to construct, use and store. I own a table saw, yet still reach for my jig to cut 4x8 sheets of plywood down to manageable size. They can also make long, straight angled cuts—something a table saw can't do.

The photos below show how to build and use one.

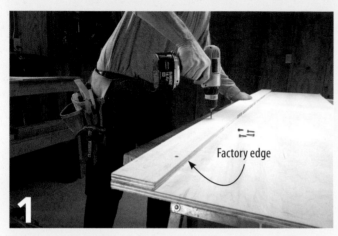

1

Use your circular saw to cut a 3- or 4-inch-wide strip from the factory edge of a sheet of plywood. You need this straight-as-an-arrow factory edge for your jig to cut straight as an arrow. Use glue and 1" drywall screws to secure this strip to a second strip of plywood at least 12-in. wide as shown.

Factory edge

2

Position the wide part of your circular saw base plate against the factory edge of the top piece, and cut through the bottom piece. You've just created a jig.

3

To use your jig, mark the piece you want cut on both ends, line up the outer edge of the jig with those marks, then screw (or clamp) the jig down. Place your saw's base plate against the edge of the upper strip and cut away.

4

Make a three or four-foot-long jig for making shorter cuts. Label your jigs so they don't wind up in the scrap pile or get used with a different saw (which might have a different size base plate).

Riley's Rocking Chair

A family heirloom with a Craftsman flare

When I started this book I conducted an informal survey, asking friends what their favorite piece of childhood furniture was. "Little rocking chair" won by a landslide. In fact, I was surprised how many people sent photos of their "little rocking chair," still being used by someone in their family. Perhaps we find solace in the metronome motion of a rocking chair throughout life because of this connection to our youth.

Figure 1

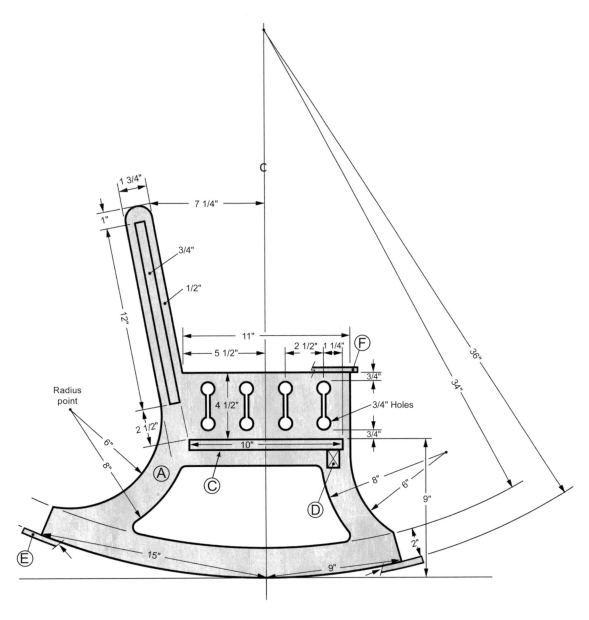

Cutting List (all refer to panel size prior to making cutouts)

Part	Dimensions	Qty
(A) Chair sides	¾" x 24" x 24"	2
(B) Back	¾" x 14" x 14"	1
(C) Seat	¾" x 14" x 10"	1
(D) Front brace	¾" x 14" x 1½"	1
(E) Rocker battens	¼" x 1¼" x 26"	2
(F) Arm rests	¼" x 1¼" x 11½"	2

Materials List

Material	Qty
¾" x 4' x 4' veneer core oak plywood	1
¼" x 1¼" x 8' oak mull strip	1

QUICK TIP

If don't own, or aren't familiar with, a biscuit joiner, you can secure the seat and back using 2" button head screws driven through the side pieces.

Figure 2

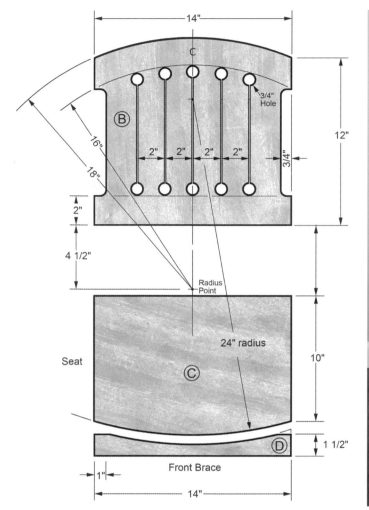

Dealing with Splintery Oak Plywood

We used oak plywood for this rocker; it's attractive, affordable and widely available—but it's also splintery because of its coarse grain. If you're not careful, it's easy to chip the edges while cutting and drilling. Here are a few tips for minimizing splinters in oak and other plywoods.

- Use a backer board to support the "exit side" of the plywood to prevent splintering when the drill bit exits. We used a woodworking Forstner bit. You can also get good results with a hole saw by drilling ¾ of the way through the front side then, using the pilot hole as a guide, finish drilling from the back side. Pay a little extra for a hole saw that has an "easy plug removal" feature. Avoid spade or paddle bits; they're likely to cause splintering even with a backer board.

- Use a fine-tooth metal cutting jigsaw blade to minimize splintering. It may take longer to make the cut, but it will be cleaner.

- When using a jigsaw or circular saw, cut your plywood good-side-down for cleanest results.

- Use a sharp utility knife to score the top layer of veneer, then cut just outside the score mark. The score mark will limit the splintering.

- Finally, to make splintering less noticeable—and to create a more attractive and touch-friendly edge—"soften" the plywood edges using a router with a round over bit.

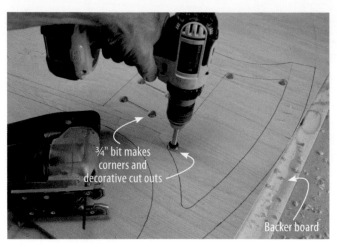

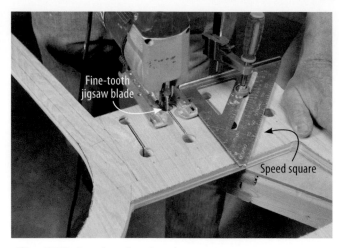

1 **LAY OUT** one side (A) of the rocking chair. Drill holes for the decorative cutouts and for the inside corners of the lower rocker cutout area.

2 **CUT** the slots for the decorative cutouts using a Speed Square as a guide. Make the first cut, move the speed square over ⅛" then make the second cut. Practice on scrap plywood beforehand.

3 **LAYOUT** the second side, using the first side as a pattern. Drill through the existing holes just deep enough to mark the holes for the second side, then remove the pattern and finish drilling.

4 **SOFTEN** the edges of the slots using sandpaper. Round over the edges of the seat, back and sides as described in the text.

This Craftsman-style rocking chair can be built from ⅓ of a sheet of ¾" plywood (handy, if you have triplets.) The details may look fancy but the cutouts are made using a drill bit and jigsaw. This project will also give you an opportunity to learn how to use a biscuit joiner, provide a few tips for bending wood and give you plenty of practice with your jigsaw.

How to Build It

Lay out one side of the rocking chair using the dimensions in Diagram A. Start by drawing your center line as a reference point and base your other measurements around that. Mark the locations of the back and seat, too; you'll need these lines for reference later on. Then layout the back (B) and seat (C),

Use a ¾" drill bit to drill the decorative holes and the rounded inside "corners" of the cutout near the bottom of the chair (Photo 1.) Use a backer board to support the back of the plywood to minimize splintering.

Use a jigsaw to cut out the parts. Cut slightly outside the lines, then use a power

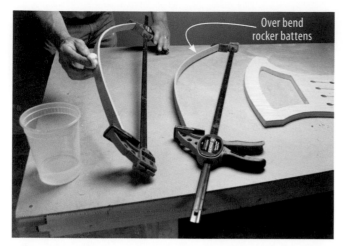

Over bend rocker battens

5 **PRE-BEND** the rocker battens (E) by repeatedly dampening them, then gradually bending them between the jaws of a bar clamp. Select straight grained wood to minimize snapping or splintering.

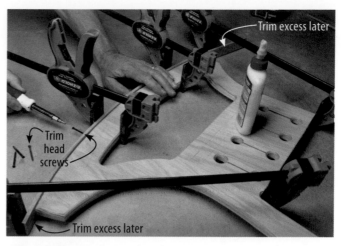

Trim excess later

Trim head screws

Trim excess later

6 **INSTALL** the rocker battens using wood glue and trim head screws. Predrill the holes using a countersink bit; this bit allows you to recess the head without splitting the wood.

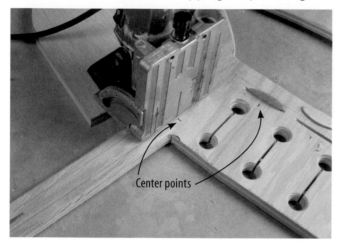

Center points

7 **CUT** the face slots for the biscuits. You may need to adjust the fence of your biscuit joiner to make these perpendicular cuts.

8 **CUT** the edge slots, making sure the slots wind up centered on the thickness of the plywood.

sander to sand up to them. Use a jigsaw guided by a Speed Square (Photo 2) to cut the slots between the holes. Practice on scrap plywood beforehand to refine your technique. Once the first side is complete, use it as a template to layout the other side (Photo 3). To mark the location of the decorative holes for the second side, drill through the finished piece, but only ¹⁄₁₆" or so into the second piece; finish boring the holes once the pattern is removed.

Use a router with a ¼" round-over bit to soften the edges of the holes and the edges

of the back, seat and sides. *Don't* rout the curved edges where rocker battens (E) will be installed, where the armrests (F) will be installed or the edges of the seat and back where biscuits will be installed.

QUICK TIP

Add fabric softener to the water when wetting the rockers; it helps the water penetrate the pores more easily, increasing flexibility.

9 **APPLY** glue to the biscuits and slots, then secure the seat and back to one of the side panels. Using "slow setting" glue will give you 10 to 15 more minutes of working time. Repeat for the second side.

10 **CLAMP** the parts tightly together. Use a square to make sure the seat is square to the side pieces before letting the glue set.

Moisten the rocker battens (E) and use clamps to "pre-bend" them (Photo 5) so they'll more easily conform to the curved plywood rockers. Over bend them (but don't break them) since they'll spring back when the clamps are removed. Let them set and dry overnight.

Use glue and trim head screws to install the rocker strips (Photo 6). Predrill holes so you don't crack the strips while installing the screws. Use lots of clamps and leave them in place overnight. Trim the overhanging parts of the strips after removing the clamps.

Mark the center points of your biscuits on the side pieces, back and seat, then use your biscuit joiner to cut the slots as shown in Photos 7 and 8. View a few YouTube tutorials to learn the basics of biscuit joinery; the system is simple and creates strong joints.

Apply glue to the biscuits and slots (Photo 9) then use lots and lots of clamps (Photo 10) to tightly sandwich the back and seat between the side pieces. Install the front brace (D) and the armrests (F). Once the glue has set, sand with progressively finer sandpaper then apply your finish of choice. We applied sanding sealer, lightly sanded the chair, then applied a light oak stain, followed by a clear water-based finish.

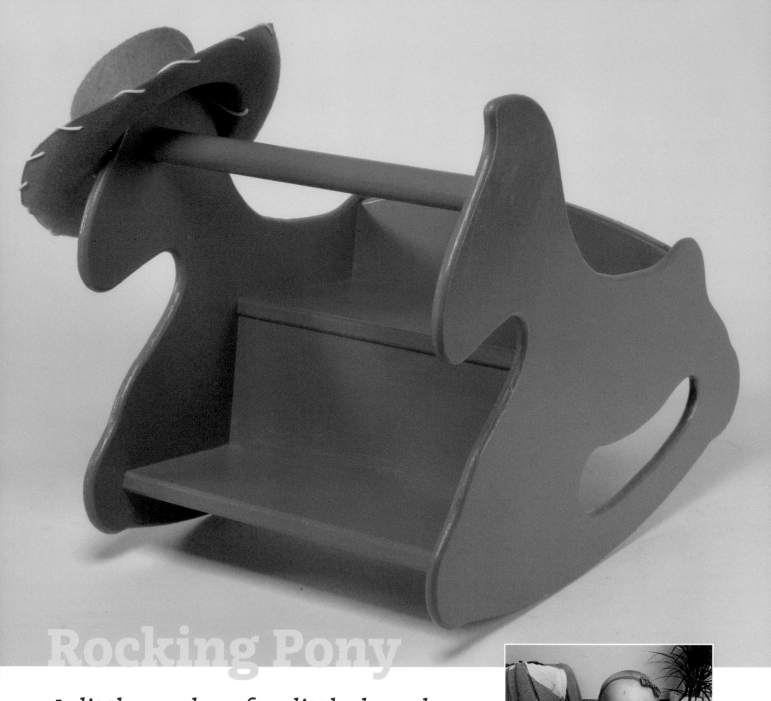

Rocking Pony

A little rocker for little hombres

Rocking *horses* are for big hombres, kids 3 or 4 years old. But this rocking pony is for little cowpokes—toddlers two and under. It's has a big seat for comfort, a solid handle for holding onto and ball-end rockers to prevent them from getting bucked off.

Like many of the other projects in this book, it leaves lots of room for do-it-yourself-imagination. Have fun varying the breed of horse, color and other things. See the "Just the right size" sidebar for more ideas.

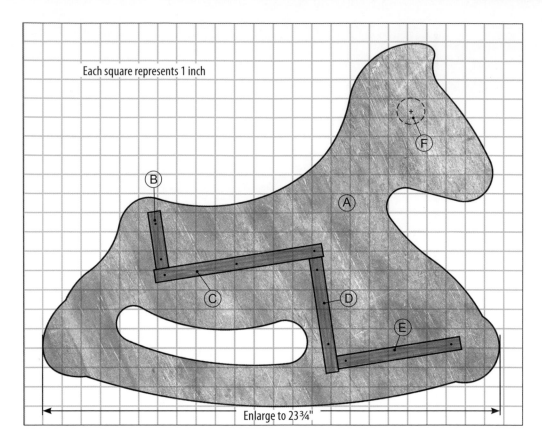

Each square represents 1 inch

(B)
(A)
(F)
(C)
(D)
(E)

Enlarge to 23¾"

Cutting List

Part	Dimensions	Qty
(A) Sides	½" x 21" x 24" plywood	2
(B) Backrest	¾" x 4½" x 14" plywood	1
(C) Seat	¾" x 9" x 14" plywood	1
(D) Leg rest	¾" x 6" x 14" plywood	1
(E) Footrest	¾" x 6½" x 14"	1
(F) Grip rod	1¼" x 14"	

Materials List

Materials	Qty
½" x 24" x 48" birch, Appleply or other plywood	1
¾" x 14" x 48" birch, Appleply, or other plywood	1
1¼" x 14" section of closet pole rod	1
Wood glue, 1⅝" trim head screws	

Note: *Appleply is made of multiple plies of ¹⁄₁₆" birch with (usually) maple veneer faces. It's so attractive it's used as an architectural, artistic or display material. Since there are no voids, the edges are attractive and often left exposed. It's more expensive than other plywoods, but, WOW!*

How to Build It

Make a photocopy of the template, then enlarge it until the squares are exactly one-inch in size. You'll eventually need to tape 6 sheets of paper together to get a full-size pattern.

Find some good old fashioned carbon paper (Photo 1) and use that to transfer the pattern onto a ½" piece of plywood (A), good face down. Trace the lines that indicate the positions of the backrest, seat, leg rest and footrest, and the marks for the screw holes.

Use a jigsaw with a fine-tooth blade (Photo 2) to cut out the first side (A). Drill

a "starter hole" for your jigsaw in the enclosed area. Cut just outside the line, then use a belt or drum sander to sand up to the line and smooth out any rough spots.

Clamp this pony cutout to the remaining ½" plywood (Photo 3) and use it as a pattern to trace the other "half" of the pony. As you proceed don't forget you're making a LEFT and a RIGHT side—and they're mirror images. Drill the screw holes for parts B, C, D and E through both pieces; and use these as reference marks for marking the positions

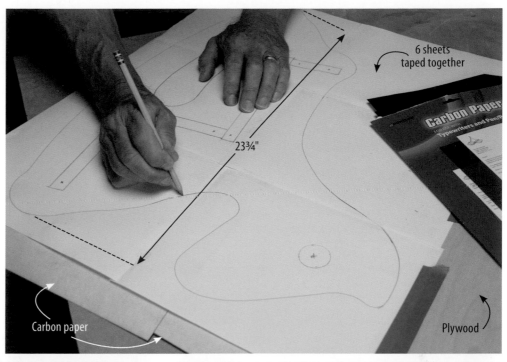

1 ENLARGE the template on a copy machine until the squares are 1" x 1". You'll need to tape 6 sheets of paper together to get the full-size pattern size. (You'll have the right size when the rocker part of the pony is 23¾" across.) Use carbon paper to transfer this pattern—including the locations of the four seat and backrest panels—onto ½" plywood.

6 sheets taped together

23¾"

Carbon paper

Plywood

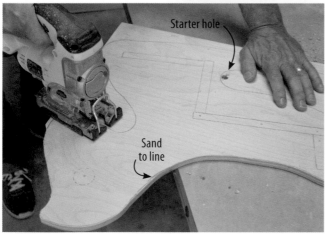

Starter hole

Sand to line

2 CUT out the shape using a jigsaw with a fine-tooth blade. Drill a starter hole in the "rocker space" so your jigsaw blade has an entry point.

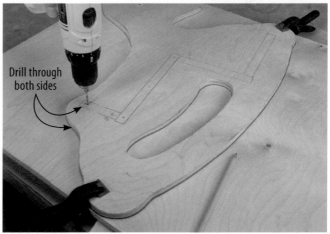

Drill through both sides

3 USE the first side panel as a template for laying out the second side panel. Drill holes for securing the seat, footrest and backrest panels through both side panels simultaneously as shown.

of those parts on the second pony half (photo 4.) Use a router with a ¼" round over bit to soften the edges of both side panels.

Cut the four pieces of plywood (B, C, D, E) that form the backrest/seat/leg rest/footrest to size. Cut a gentle arc along the top of the backrest. Use a router to soften the top edge of B, the front and back edges of C and the front edge of E. Use the lines on one of the

side panels (A) as a guide for assembling the four boards (Photo 5). Use glue and trim head drywall screws to secure the four panels to one another, *then* use the layout marks on the side panels to position this 4-board assembly and secure it with trim head screws. Install the grip rod (G) as shown in Photo 6. Apply paint or a clear finish of choice. If you're feeling artistic, draw in eyes, saddle and other features.

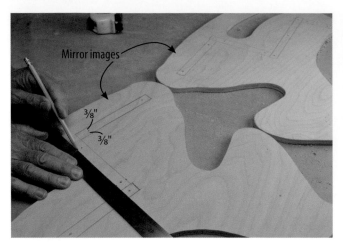

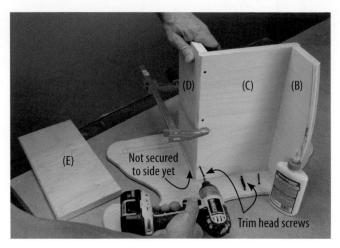

4 **DRAW** the positions of the backrest (B), seat (C), leg rest (D) and footrest (E) onto the second side, using the holes drilled in the previous photo as guides.

5 **SECURE** panels B, C, D and E to one another using glue and trim head screws, then screw this entire assembly to the two side panels.

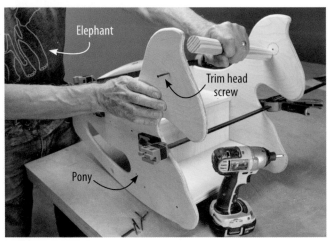

6 **INSTALL** the grip rod (F). Apply the paint or clear finish of your choice.

Build a Rocking Car, Dinosaur or Turtle

We provide a pattern for a rocking pony—but not every kid is an equine lover. Maybe he or she is fascinated by fire trucks. Or dogs. Or dinosaurs. If so, you can rock their world by making one of those too. How? Let's use dinosaurs as an example.

Go online and punch in "Dinosaur Silhouette Images." You'll get page after page of dinosaur silhouette images. Not all of them are "rocking material," but select one that has possibilities, and print it out. Doodle with a pencil to see if the rocker configuration from the pony will fit and look okay on the dinosaur. Sketch in the 4-part seat assembly and see if *that* will fit—and if it does, see if the seat can be centered so the rocking dinosaur will be evenly balanced. If you think you're onto something, blow it up on your copy machine until it's about 24" long, then follow the same steps we show for building the pony. This is more art than science, not every pattern will work and it's a fair amount of screwing around. But my, won't his or her eyes light up when they see a rocking Tyrannosaurus Rex?

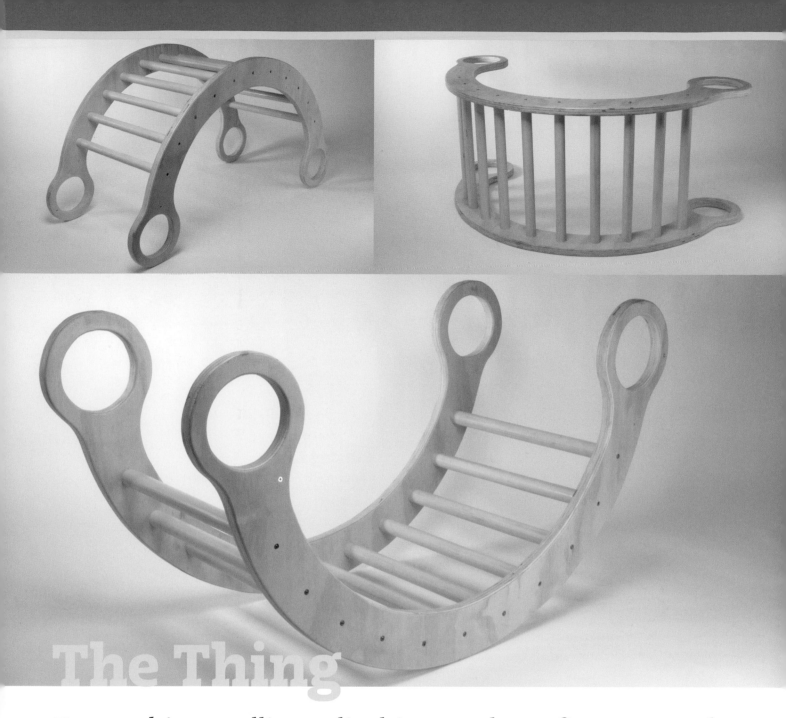

The Thing

For rocking, rolling, climbing and goofing around

Kids love rocking and rolling, climbing and crawling, hiding and playing; The Thing provides a one-stop shop for all these activities and more. Perhaps the coolest feature is The Thing's propensity to inspire creative play and physical activity.

It can be used inside and out; right side up, upside down and on its side; by one or two kids; and by kids of all ages. Since this versatility means it can be used in crazy ways, set the ground rules before your kids cut loose on The Thing.

Figure 1

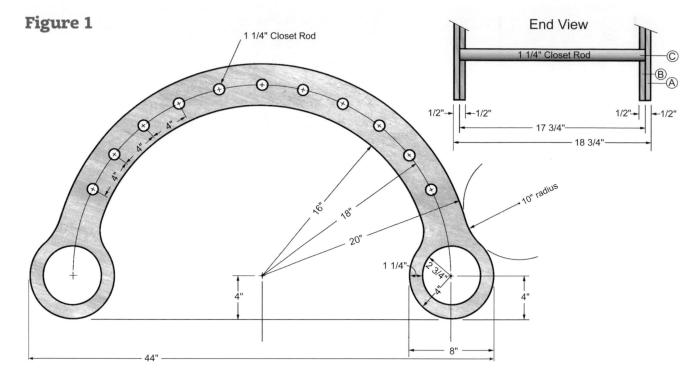

How to Build It

Establish a center point as shown in Diagram A, then swing three large arcs—one for the inside curve, one for the outside and one to mark the centers of the rungs. Use a hand held compass to draw the smaller circular handholds (Photo 1). Trace around the bottom of a drywall bucket to establish the gentle arc connecting the handholds and the main arc. Mark the positions of the rungs on the center arch. Check and double check your dimensions; you'll use this first arch as a template for the other three.

Use a jigsaw (Photo 2) to cut the arch to shape. The relief cut allows you to remove cutoffs in smaller, more manageable pieces. Drill starter holes in the hand holds to give your jigsaw blade an entry point. Use a belt sander and drum sander (shown in Photo 6) to smooth the edges. If you own an oscillating drum sander, this is the perfect time to use it.

Trace around this first arch to create outlines for the other three arches (Photo 3). "Nest them" as shown so you can cut all four pieces from one sheet of plywood. Cut 'em out.

Cutting List

Part	Dimension	Qty
(A) Solid arches	½" x 24" x 44" (approx.)	2
(B) Arches with rung holes	½" x 24" x 44" (approx.)	2
(C) Rungs	1¼" x 17¾" closet rod	11

Materials List

Material	Qty
½" x 4' x 8' plywood	1
1¼" x 10' closet rod	2

Drill the eleven rung holes in two of the arches (Photo 4) using a 1¼" Forstner bit. Once you've drilled the holes in one arch, lay that over the other arch and use it as a guide for drilling those holes. Glue up the arches—one with holes, one without—to create each side. Use clamps—lots of them—and ¾" screws to hold the pieces tightly against one another.

Once the glue has dried, sand the doubled-up arches and smooth the curves with power sanders. Use a router and a ¼" round-over bit to soften all the edges.

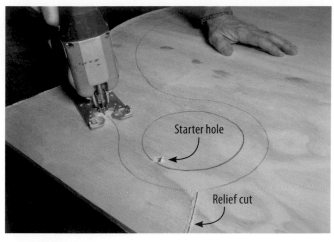

1 SWING three large arcs to layout the first rocker. Use a tape measure and pencil for the large arcs and a hand held compass to mark the hand holds.

2 CUT the rocker to shape using a jigsaw. Make a series of relief cuts so you can remove scraps in manageable size piece. Drill starter holes in the handhold openings to give your jigsaw blade entry points.

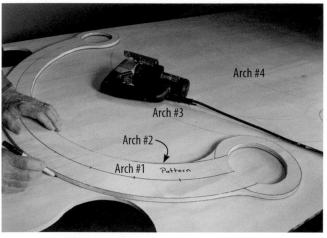

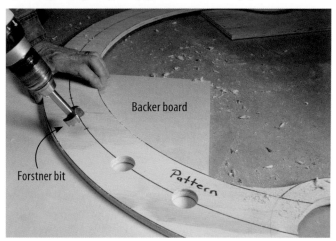

3 TRACE around your first arch to create three more. By "nesting" them as shown, you can cut all four rockers from a single sheet of plywood.

4 DRILL 1¼" holes for the rungs in two of the arches. Use a backer board to prevent "blow out" when the bit breaks through the back of the plywood.

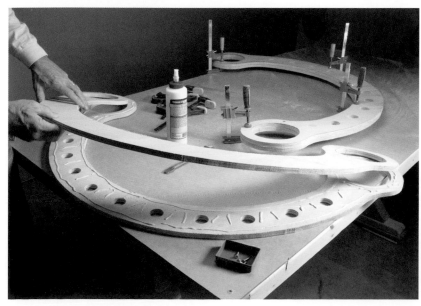

5 GLUE up the arches in pairs; one with holes, one without. Use clamps and ¾" screws to draw the pieces tightly together.

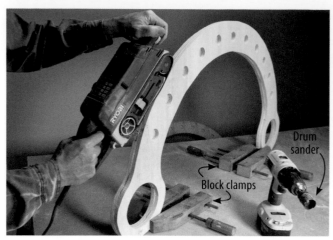

6 **USE** a belt sander to even up the outside and inside curves. Use a drum sander chucked into your drill to smooth areas your belt sander can't reach. Round over the edges with a router.

Labels in photo: Drum sander, Block clamps

7 **ASSEMBLE** The Thing. Apply glue and use screws to secure the rungs into the holes of one arch then, using clamps to hold the arches together as you work, install the other ends. A helper can come in mighty handy here.

Finally, install the rungs. Paint them ahead of time if you want a colorful "Thing." Apply glue to one end of each rung, insert the ends into the holes of one arch assembly, then install screws to suck the rungs deeply into each hole. Apply glue then insert the other end of each rung into the opposing arch. Start at one end and gradually work your way around to the other (Photo 7). Use clamps to squeeze the two halves together as you go. If you enlist a helper, this will go easier. When all of the rung ends are inserted in the other arch, use screws to draw them tighter, too.

Apply two coats of protective polyurethane finish, then rock and roll.

The Best Big Bit

There are at least three kinds of bits—spade bits, hole saws and Forstner bits—you can use for drilling big holes. They all have their pros and cons. Spade bits (sometimes known as paddle bits) are inexpensive, but tend to bore less uniform holes—and if an edge "catches," it can cause your drill to wrench your wrist in a serious way. Hole saws are another option, but removing the little circular cutouts from the bit can be time consuming and frustrating. We opted to use a Forstner bit; they cost more than the others, but bore a nice clean hole and create minimum "blow out" when the bit exits the plywood (as long as you use a backer board.)

Imperial to Metric Conversion

Inches	mm*	inches	mm*	inches	mm
1/64	0.40	33/64	13.10	1	25.4
1/32	0.79	17/32	13.49	2	50.8
3/64	1.19	35/64	13.89	3	76.2
1/16	1.59	9/16	14.29	4	101.6
5/64	1.98	37/64	14.68	5	127.0
3/32	2.38	19/32	15.08	6	152.4
7/64	2.78	39/64	15.48	7	177.8
1/8	3.18	5/8	15.88	8	203.2
9/64	3.57	41/64	16.27	9	228.6
5/32	3.97	21/32	16.67	10	254.0
11/64	4.37	43/64	17.07	11	279.4
3/16	4.76	11/16	17.46	12	304.8
13/64	5.16	45/64	17.86	13	330.2
7/32	5.56	23/32	18.26	14	355.6
15/64	5.95	47/64	18.65	15	381.0
1/4	6.35	3/4	19.05	16	406.4
17/64	6.75	49/64	19.45	17	431.8
9/32	7.14	25/32	19.84	18	457.2
19/64	7.54	51/64	20.24	19	482.6
5/16	7.94	13/16	20.64	20	508.0
21/64	8.33	53/64	21.03	21	533.4
11/32	8.73	27/32	21.43	22	558.8
23/64	9.13	55/64	21.83	23	584.2
3/8	9.53	7/8	22.23	24	609.6
25/64	9.92	57/64	22.62	25	635.0
13/32	10.32	29/32	23.02	26	660.4
27/64	10.72	59/64	23.42	27	685.8
7/16	11.11	15/16	23.81	28	711.2
29/64	11.51	61/64	24.21	29	736.6
15/32	11.91	31/32	24.61	30	762.0
31/64	12.30	63/64	25.00	31	787.4
1/2	12.70	1 inch	25.40	32	812.8

*Rounded to the nearest 0.01 mm

About Spike

Spike Carlsen is an editor, author, carpenter and wood-worker, who's been immersed in the world of wood and woodworking for 40 years. He's author of the award-winning *A Splintered History of Wood: Belt Sander Races, Blind Woodworkers and Baseball Bats, Ridiculously Simple Furniture Projects, Woodworking FAQ, The Backyard Homestead Book of Building Projects* and *Cabin Lessons*.

He is former Executive Editor of *Family Handyman* magazine where he wrote hundreds of articles on home improvement and woodworking, and oversaw the creation of the *Revised Reader's Digest, Complete Do-It-Yourself Manual*. He's made appearances on the CBS Early Show, HGTV and Modern Marvels and written for *Men's Health, Fine Homebuilding, The Minneapolis Star Tribune* and many other publications.

Prior to becoming an editor he worked as a carpenter for 15 years, and ran his own construction and remodeling company. He and his wife Kat have five children, nine grandchildren and one very old house in historic Stillwater, Minnesota. In his spare time he enjoys biking, woodworking with kids, traveling and spending time at their Lake Superior cabin (which he also built.)

Find out more at spikecarlsen.com.

Spike and granddaughter Priya discuss furniture design.

More Great Woodworking Books from Linden Publishing

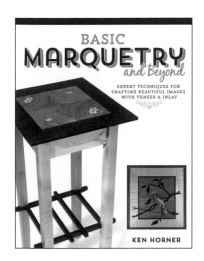

Basic Marquetry and Beyond
176 pp. $24.95
978-1-610352-49-9

Carving for Kids
104 pp. $16.95
978-1-933502-02-1

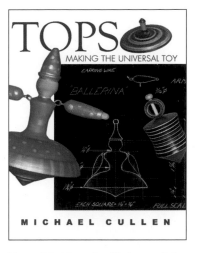

Tops: Making the Universal Toy
128 pp. $17.95
978-1-933502-17-5

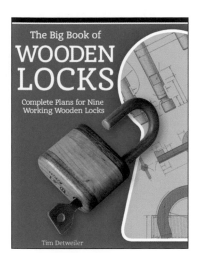

The Big Book of Wooden Locks
160 pp. $24.95
978-1-610352-22-2

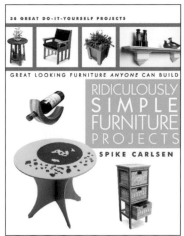

*Ridiculously Simple
Furniture Projects*
122 pp. $19.95
978-1-610350-04-4

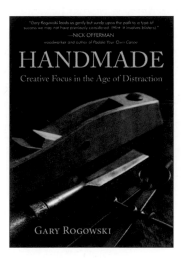

*Handmade: Creative Focus
in the Age of Distraction*
184 pp. $18.95
978-1-610353-14-4

More Great Woodworking Books from Linden Publishing

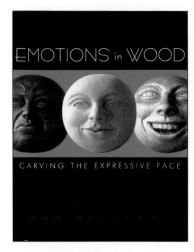

*Emotions in Wood:
Carving the Expressive Face*
128 pp. $19.95
978-1-933502-16-8

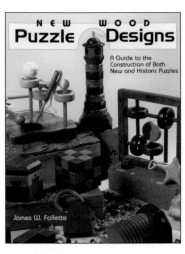

New Wood Puzzle Designs
96 pp. $21.95
978-0-941936-57-6

*Doormaking: Materials,
Techniques and Projects
for Building Your First Door*
144 pp. $26.95
978-1-610352-91-8

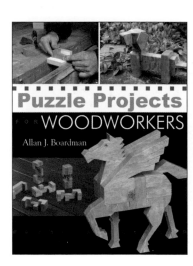

*Puzzle Projects
for Woodworkers*
96 pp. $19.95
978-1-933502-11-3

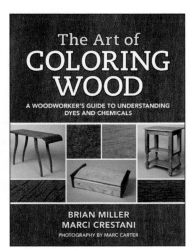

*The Art of Coloring Wood:
A Woodworker's Guide
to Understanding Dyes
and Chemicals*
144 pp. $24.95
978-1-610353-05-2

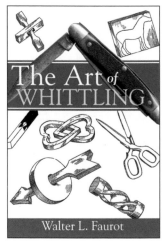

The Art of Whittling
91 pp. $9.95
978-1-933502-07-6